The Pourcel Brothers

Cookbook

MANAGING EDITORS: Stephen Bateman
and Pierre-Jean Furet

EDITOR:
Brigitte Éveno

ART DIRECTOR:
Florence Cailly (China)

PRODUCTION: Claire Leleu

This edition first published in English in 2004 by Hachette
Illustrated UK, Octopus Publishing Group Ltd., 2–4 Heron Quays,
London E14 4JP
English translation © Octopus Publishing Group Ltd.

Translation from French: First Edition Translations Ltd., in
conjunction with Book Production Consultants plc, Cambridge

ISBN-13: 978-1-84430-099-0
ISBN-10: 1-84430-099-4

Jacques & Laurent Pourcel

Pourcel Brothers
Cookbook

our recipes from La Compagnie des Comptoirs

Photographs: Bernhard Winkelmann

Stylist: Valérie Lhomme

Project editor: Philippe Lamboley

Editorial associate: Sophie Brissaud

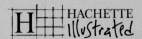
HACHETTE Illustrated

Contents

Introduction

Roots in Languedoc

How do you know where you belong when you're from the Western part of the French Mediterranean South?

You can stay right there and get to know the intricate details of your own country; you can learn, from two sips of wine, how to tell grapes from one patch of a Languedocian vineyard from the next one; you can spot the local thyme and sage in the fragrance of a picpoul rosé; love both the quiet, wide-open sandy seaside between Camargue and Catalonia and the white, sun-baked, windswept limestone heights of a goat-ridden, gamey hinterland, where chestnuts and cèpe mushrooms grow; you can sharpen your senses of smell and taste, anticipating the truffle season, around November. Simply, you can just let yourself be from Languedoc. We know how to do this, but we have also learned that the further away you travel from your origins, the clearer and more precise they appear to you at a distance. Since we have entered the world of haute cuisine and the status of star-chefdom, we have been constantly navigating between these two poles: our Southern French roots and the call of faraway destinations. Perhaps because we are twin brothers we find no contradiction in this dichotomy. Being two allows us sometimes to be twice as strong as one would be, and sometimes to be like one person in two different places.

So we let our dreams take us along the coast

Above and left: *laticed shutters, golden colours and culinary escape in Montpellier and La Grande-Motte.*

Right: *the restaurant in Montpelier, created and opened in 2000, marked the beginning of La Compagnie des Comptoirs.*

and across the sea, through Spain to Africa, and via Greece and Turkey to the Middle and Far East; such is the natural impulse of being born in Languedoc, close to the antique seaports of Marseille, Agde, Sète and Barcelona: the South calls you. Our region is like a balcony which opens out onto the sea, and allows your imagination to take in the whole Mediterranean in a wide fan-shaped movement. Marseille offers it all in a nutshell, with a plentiful North African population colouring and shaping the city's culture and destiny, as Greek, Roman and Spanish settlers have done long before them. Beyond Spain, Italy and the three countries of Maghreb – Morocco, Algeria and Tunisia – lies the East of North Africa, the West of Asia and the many Greek islands which appear like stepping-stones to the East. For thousands of years, this region has been a melting pot, a cultural and commercial community, a combination of tastes, colours and smells that form the character of the Mediterranean cuisines. This is our natural element; a little mobility was all it took to grasp it fully. Following that movement, it was easy to take the dream further: to India, Southeast Asia, China and Japan.

We belong both here and there. We are not affiliated to any school and do not feel tied down by tradition or past influences. We prefer to be ourselves, to look towards the future; Mediterranean at heart, but something different as well.

La Compagnie des Comptoirs in France

Since we and our friend and associate, Olivier Château, created our first gourmet restaurant *Le Jardin des Sens* in 1988, we have constantly promoted the produce and the cuisine of our region, although other regions – the Mediterranean, Asia, the Indian Ocean islands – have obviously influenced our cooking as well. However, we felt a strong desire to explore the world, and after our restaurant *Le Jardin des Sens* received its third Michelin star, in 1997, this exploration began to take shape as with the formation of *La Compagnie des Comptoirs* and the opening of new restaurants in France and abroad.

La Compagnie des Comptoirs is the embodiment of three ideas that we cherish. The first is to travel with your mind and senses through the cuisine and culture of a region. Second is to gather people in a pleasant, relaxed, modern, relatively inexpensive place, where you serve them delicious food and make them happy (an echo of our own natural sense of friendship and conviviality). Third is a fascination with the exotic culture of colonial

Europe, the spice trade between West and East Indies, the Far East, the Indian Ocean, the South Seas, the New World. It is the convergence of many desires into one single aim: making good cooking more fun, more accessible, and a better stimulant for the imagination.

The first *Compagnie des Comptoirs* was created in December 2000, in Montpellier, facing *Le Jardin des Sens*. We asked the interior designer Imaad Rahmouni – who follows us through every new *Compagnie* – to produce a warm atmosphere, both modern and timeless, with exotic woods, carved Indonesian screens, antique sea maps, leather-bound books and etchings from colonial histories, like a sensorial echo of the East India Company. Outside the restaurant, a large patio is centered around a water pond, a feature that all *Compagnies des Comptoirs* have in common.

The concept of the *Compagnies* also extends itself to the food: generous, light, colourful and inspired by the East and the South – but mostly through a constant renewing of our imagination – it is meant to provoke satisfaction and excitement at a moderate price.

One year later, a second *Compagnie* was created in Avignon, in the extraordinary setting of an 18th-century convent. We decided to give this place a more modern look than that of the first *Compagnie*. Soon

afterwards, with the third *Compagnie*, *Effet Mer* – on the coast near Montpellier – we renewed the concept of the beach restaurant. *Effet Mer* is a long structure divided into several rooms and lounges by carved teakwood panels, and shaded by a huge sand-coloured awnings. With your feet in the sand while you are eating or having a drink, the sense of the tropical East is ever present in the sea wind that gently plays through the saffron-coloured awnings of Balinese four-posted beds and the palm trees and cacti of a seashore garden.

While *La Compagnie des Comptoirs* is our poetic venture into the concept of travel, our cuisine has been doing some real travelling. Soon after the first *Compagnie* opened in Montpellier, our brasserie *Sens et Saveurs* opened above the Tokyo Imperial Gardens.

Left: *Jacques and Laurent Pourcel.*

Above:
Olivier Château, Jacques and Laurent Pourcel's partner.

Above:
Effet Mer is a long buiding divided into separate rooms by teak partitions, and shaded by a large sand coloured awning.

Spring 2004 saw the opening of another one of our restaurants in Bangkok, followed by a further opening in Shanghai in Autumn 2004. We remain particularly fond of all our *Compagnies*, in which we put a lot of ourselves and some of our most cherished principles.

W!Sens, the *Compagnie* in London

Our travels have taken us primarily to the South and East. By comparison, we got to know Northern Europe rather late. To us, London was a gradual discovery, over the last few years. From one short visit to another, we took a liking to this beautiful metropolis. What we found there was not only the capital of England but indeed the whole world, contained in one large, lively city. The combination of the British lifestyle – with its passion for comfort, peacefulness and elegance – and the cosmopolitan culture inherited from the former colonial empire fascinated us right from the start. While it is as beautiful as its near neighbour Paris, in London everything is on a more human scale and it is buzzing with life.

The street culture, the theatres, museums and galleries, and of course the food and wine: in London, wherever you stand, there is always something to do, to see, to taste, to share; something new and exciting around the corner. Cafés, restaurants, theatres are all brimming with vitality and creativity. We greatly enjoy this openness, youthfulness and diversity, particularly in the culinary field. In London, you may taste excellent and genuine ethnic foods – Chinese, Indian, Thai, Japanese, West Indian – and in gourmet cuisine and British food, many new and talented local chefs have reinstated, during the last decade, London's worldwide reputation as a city of fine eating.

The creation of a new *Compagnie des Comptoirs* in London seemed to us like a logical decision. Some of our British clients in

Montpellier and Avignon urged us to open a *Compagnie* in London, we finally followed their advice and made the move. The concept of the *Compagnie* seems particularly well suited to the cosmopolitan, pleasure-loving and lively atmosphere of London. No translation is necessary between the Languedocian South, dreaming of Mediterranean and Oriental escapades, and London, open and welcoming to people from all directions and from all nations. For *W'Sens*, we adapted the concept of *La Compagnie des Comptoirs* to a whole new environment and clientele. The restaurant is located in an elegant building in beautiful Waterloo Place, part of the historical heart of London. It has a total area of 800 square meters on three levels. In accordance with the concept of *La Compagnie des Comptoirs*, there is a lounge bar on the ground floor, where the main dining-room is also located and a large staircase leading to a mezzanine. Once again, we asked Imaad Rahmouni to design this venue, with a stress on timelessness and memorabilia of colonial splendour. We want this décor to last for years, knowing that what is fashionable today will be out of fashion tomorrow.

The menu, predictably, reflects the fourfold concept of the *Compagnie*: Vegetables, the South, the East, and Desserts. Through our choice of dishes, we are trying to reach and satisfy the widest possible audience. And we

are confident that Londoners will love to travel with us to the colourful regions of taste that we have already had so much fun exploring.

W'SENS
La Compagnie des Comptoirs
12 Waterloo Place
St James's
London
SW1

www.lacompagniedescomptoirs.com

Opposite page, top Left: *vaulted ceilings and pale stone in this ancient 17th century cloister, which since 2001 has housed La compagnie des Comptoirs in Avignon.*

bottom right: *Exterior of W'Sens, La Compagnie des Comptoirs in the heart of London.*

Twelve early summer vegetables, herb dressing and crushed peanuts

To serve 4

For cooking the vegetables
1 piece fresh ginger
1 piece fresh galingale
1 dried chilli pepper (optional)
500 ml (18 fl oz) cold water
100 ml (3½ fl oz) grape seed oil
250 g (9 oz) unsalted butter
juice of 1 lime
salt

Early summer vegetables
4 'petals' of slow-baked tomato (see recipe on p. 60)
2 baby violet artichokes
4 spears of green asparagus (wild if possible)
4 red radishes
2 large, bulbous spring onions
2 baby courgettes
4 florets of cauliflower
1 stick celery
2 very small, young bulbs of fennel
½ Chinese cabbage (Chinese leaves)
90 g (3 oz) baby broad beans, shelled, inner skins removed
8 snow-peas or mange-touts

To assemble the dish
A few leaves each of fresh Thai basil, coriander, chives and mint
Toasted, crushed peanuts

Peel the ginger and the galingale. Finely chop the ginger; mince or grate the galingale. Crumble the dried chilli pepper.

Cooking the vegetables

Set the tomato petals aside for garnishing the finished dish. Peel and wash all the vegetables as appropriate and cut them into small, differently shaped pieces. Cook each type separately (except for the broad beans and snow-peas or mange-touts) in approximately 50 ml (2 fl oz) water with ½ tsp grape seed oil, a little ginger, galingale and chilli pepper, 1–2 tsps butter and a pinch of salt for each batch. Add a squeeze of lime juice to the water in which you cook the artichokes and the celery. Cook the broad beans and the snow-peas or mange-touts separately, in boiling, salted water, as directed for the green vegetables at the top of facing page, page 19, until they are tender but still crisp. Plunge into iced water to refresh so they will keep their colour; drain.

Assembling the dish

Drain off the flavoured cooking juices from all the vegetables (see note on page 26 at end of recipe) and reserve in a bowl. Keep hot. Arrange all the vegetables on fairly deep plates or shallow soup dishes; decorate each serving with a tomato petal. Add more flavour if needed to the reserved cooking juices, using grape seed oil, salt and lime juice. Use an electric whisk to blend this dressing; add the fresh herb leaves. Sprinkle over the vegetables. Top with a sprinkling of coarsely chopped or crushed peanuts.

This dish, with its echoes of Thailand, is prepared in much the same way as the Greek vegetable salad on page 20, but the two recipes use very different spices and flavours, giving a choice between Mediterranean and Asian interpretations of mixed-vegetable salads.

Vegetable medley on puff pastry base with pesto and black olive vinaigrette

Cooking the vegetables

Clean and prepare all the vegetables. Cook each type separately in boiling water until tender but still crisp, allowing 30 g (scant 2 tbsps or 1 oz) salt per 1 litre (1¾ pints) water for the green vegetables (snow-peas or mange-touts, asparagus, French beans) and 12 g (scant 1 tbsp or scant ½ oz) salt per 1 litre (1¾ pints) water for the other vegetables (carrots, turnips, spring onions, artichokes). Drain each batch of vegetables and plunge into a large bowl of iced water to refresh and 'fix' the colour.

Cooking the puff pastry

Preheat the oven to 220 °C (gas mark 7–8). Roll out the pastry into a thin sheet and use a pastry cutter to cut out 4 discs of the required size, according to preference, and use the prongs of a fork to prick the surface of the pastry. Transfer to a prepared baking sheet; place a second, matching baking sheet on top of the pastry discs and bake for 12 minutes in the oven. Halfway through this time, remove the top baking sheet and allow the pastry to finish baking and turn pale golden brown. Set aside.

Pesto dressing

Place the basil leaves, the garlic cloves, olive oil and a little salt in a food processor or blender. Process until smoothly blended. Transfer to a bowl and clean the food processor or blender, ready to make the black olive dressing.

Tapenade (black olive) dressing

Place all the ingredients for this in the blender or food processor and process at high speed. Adjust seasoning to taste.

Assembling the dish

Reheat all the vegetables together with a little olive oil in a heavy-bottomed saucepan or casserole dish; when they have reheated, add a generous tablespoon of pesto and stir; season with salt and pepper to taste.

Spoon a little pesto into a saucer and roll the cherry tomatoes in it.

Reheat the pastry rounds gently for a few minutes and place one in the centre of each of 4 plates. Spread a little tapenade over each pastry round, then arrange one-quarter of the vegetables on top; decorate with a pesto-flavoured tomato. Garnish each serving with a few rocket leaves. Dribble a thread of pesto around the outer edge of the pastry; repeat this last process with the black olive dressing.

> This is another recipe that makes the most of our Mediterranean repertoire (the flavours of pesto and tapenade are typical of this region), providing a medley of sun-drenched tastes heaped on crisp and tender flaky pastry.

To serve 4

1 packet ready-made puff pastry

For the vegetable medley
120 g (4 oz) baby carrots
120 g (4 oz) baby turnips
100 g (3½ oz) snow-peas or mange-touts
120 g (4 oz) large spring onions
150 g (5 oz) green asparagus
80 g (3 oz) baby violet artichokes
80 g (3 oz) French beans
coarse sea salt

For the pesto
leaves from a large bunch of fresh basil
3 or 4 cloves of garlic, peeled
250 ml (9 fl oz) olive oil
salt

For the tapenade (black olive) dressing
250 g (9 oz) tinned black olives, stoned
60 g (2 oz) capers (in vinegar)
1 or 2 cloves of garlic, peeled
150 ml (5 fl oz) olive oil
4 salted anchovies
salt, freshly ground pepper

To assemble the dish
olive oil
4 ripe red cherry tomatoes
100 g (3½ oz) rocket, rinsed and dried in a cloth
salt, freshly ground pepper

Vegetarian foods and vegetables

vegetarian first courses

Greek mixed vegetable salad, dried orange zest marinade, sugar-glazed orange slices

For the dried orange
250 ml (9 fl oz) water
150 g (5 oz) sugar
1 orange for the sugar-glazed
orange slices
1 orange for the baked peel

For the vegetables
2 baby carrots
2 white button mushrooms
½ small celeriac root
4 thin, green asparagus
spears, ideally wild
2 thin baby leeks
2 baby turnips
2 baby fennel bulbs
2 baby courgettes
2 baby globe artichokes
4 cauliflower florets
50 g (2 oz) fresh girolle
mushrooms
8 small mange-tout pea pods
1½ litres (2 pints 4 fl oz) water
or fresh chicken stock
100 ml (3½ fl oz) olive oil
salt, whole coriander seeds
1 lemon

**For the Greek-style
dressing**
olive oil
juice of 2 lemons
juice of 1 orange
salt, freshly ground pepper

To assemble the dish
4 slow-baked tomato 'petals'
(see recipe on p. 54)
4 very small bunches of fresh
basil

Rinse, peel and trim all the vegetables as appropriate and cut them into small, differently shaped pieces.

Sugar-glazed orange slices

Make a sugar syrup by bringing the sugar and water to the boil. Use a mandoline cutter or a very sharp knife to cut an unpeeled orange into very thin, round slices. Add these to the sugar syrup and simmer gently for 1 hour. When they are nearly done, preheat the oven to 110 °C (gas mark 3–4).
Drain the orange slices (keep the syrup). Cover a baking sheet or shallow baking tray with non-stick greaseproof or silicone paper; spread out the orange slices on it in a single layer and dry out in the oven for 1 hour 20 minutes. They should become as crunchy as crisps.
Use a potato peeler to peel off the zest of the orange (just the peel, no white pith). Simmer the strips of zest in the reserved sugar syrup for 1 hour, then drain well and spread out on fresh non-stick greaseproof or silicone paper to dry out in the oven, following the method used for the orange slices. When the zest has completely dried out, transfer to the food processor and process to a powder. Set aside.

Cooking the vegetables

With the exception of the mange-touts, cook all the vegetables separately, using 100 ml (3½ fl oz) water or chicken stock, ½ tsp olive oil, a pinch of salt and a few coriander seeds for each batch, until they are tender but still crisp. Do not drain. Sprinkle a little lemon juice over the baby turnips, the artichokes, girolles and celeriac. Set aside.

Cook the mange-touts in salted water until tender but crisp, in fast-boiling water (allow 30 g (scant 2 tbsps or 1 oz) salt for each 1 litre (1¾ pints). Drain and refresh in iced water to 'set' their colour.

Greek dressing

Drain all the cooked vegetables, pouring their cooking liquid (not that from the mange-touts) into a bowl. Mix this liquid with a little more olive oil and add salt, freshly ground pepper, lemon and orange juice to taste.

Assembling the dish

Arrange a similar selection of vegetables on each of 4 fairly deep dishes or in shallow soup plates, decorating each serving with a tomato 'petal'.
Sprinkle each portion with some of the orange zest powder and with the dressing; decorate with a crunchy orange round and with a very small bunch of fresh basil.

When cooking each type of vegetable, do not allow the liquid to boil dry but merely to reduce. When the reduced cooking juices are mixed together, they will form the Greek-style dressing. There is nothing to stop you varying this recipe, choosing other vegetables, increasing or decreasing the quantity of something or other...

Crisp-fried wonton skins layered with stir-fried vegetables, herb-flavoured oil

For the mushroom sauce
100 g (3½ oz) granulated or caster sugar
120 ml (4 fl oz) rice wine vinegar (see note in method)
200 g (7 oz) fresh shitake mushrooms, cleaned and trimmed
500 ml (18 fl oz) vegetable stock
salt

For the herb-flavoured oil
small bunch of fresh chives
small bunch fresh coriander
100 ml (3½ fl oz) olive oil
salt

For the vegetables
160 g (5½–6 oz) Chinese leaves (Chinese cabbage)
160 g (5–6 oz) pak choy (see note at end of method)
200 g (7 oz) fresh shitake mushrooms
240 g (½ lb) carrots
2 medium-sized onions
40 g (1½ oz) fresh ginger, peeled
1 clove garlic, peeled
generous 1 tbsp sesame seed oil
salt, freshly ground pepper

To assemble the dish
1 packet Chinese wonton skins (thin pastry squares, see note at end of method)
1 litre (1¾ pints) peanut oil for frying

vegetarian first courses

Mushroom sauce

Pour the sugar into a heavy-bottomed saucepan and cook gently without adding any water until it melts and caramelizes. When it is golden brown, pour in the rice wine vinegar and bring to the boil. Add the shitake mushrooms, followed by the vegetable stock. Cover and leave to simmer for 45 minutes, then transfer to the blender and process, adding seasoning if necessary. Pour into a saucepan and keep warm.

Herb-flavoured oil

Rinse and dry the chives and coriander. Take the leaves off the coriander stalks and process both herbs with the olive oil and a little salt in the blender. Pour into a bowl.

The vegetables

Cut the Chinese cabbage, the pak choy and the shitake mushrooms into fairly large pieces; slice the carrots thinly at an angle of 45° (on the slant) and chop the onions finely. Crush the ginger and the garlic or chop very finely indeed. Pour the sesame seed oil into a large fireproof casserole dish or wok and, when hot, add the vegetables; stir-fry over a high heat until they are tender but still very crisp. Add a little mushroom sauce before setting aside.

Assembling the dish

Heat the peanut oil in a deep fryer to a temperature of 160 °C. Fry the wonton skins until they are crisp and pale golden brown; remove from the oil and drain on paper towels.

Place a fried wonton skin on each plate, heap up some vegetables on it, cover with another wonton skin and surround with a ribbon of mushroom sauce. Sprinkle a little herb-flavoured oil over the top wonton.

> You will find all the ingredients you need for this recipe (the vegetables, rice wine vinegar, sesame seed oil, wonton skins etc.) in a good Oriental grocery shop or in the better supermarkets. Pak choy or bok choy is a type of Chinese cabbage with fleshy white ribs or stalks and green leaves, rather like a small, squat version of silver beet or Swiss chard.

Fluffy oat cakes, braised girolle mushrooms, hazelnut oil

For the oat cakes

Preheat the oven to 180 °C (gas mark 6). Bring the milk to the boil with the butter in a saucepan. Season with salt and pepper; stir in the rolled oats and leave to stand for 20 minutes. When this mixture has cooled and is lukewarm, separate the egg yolks from their whites. Stir the yolks into the oat 'porridge'; whisk the egg whites until they form peaks and fold gently into the oat mixture in a large mixing bowl, using a spatula.

Transfer a quarter of this mixture into each of 4 deep round, non-stick moulds 7–8 cm (3 in) in diameter (dariole moulds are ideal); the moulds should be three-quarters full. Bake for approximately 30 minutes in the oven, then turn out and keep hot.

Braised girolles

Clean the girolles. Heat the butter in a heavy-bottomed saucepan and sauté the girolles briefly over a high heat. Season with salt and pepper and drain in a sieve placed over the bowl; keep the juices. Return this juice to the pan and cook, uncovered, until it has reduced to a thicker, syrupy consistency. Beat in the hazelnut oil with a hand-held electric whisk. Keep warm.

Herb salad

Pick over the herbs, rinse them and blot dry. Make the vinaigrette by mixing the salt and pepper with the vinegar, then add the hazelnut oil in a thin stream while beating energetically. Sprinkle a little of this dressing over the herbs just before assembling the dish.

Assembling the dish

Place an oat cake in the centre of each plate. Top each oat cake with some girolles (make sure these are really hot), then place some of the mixed-herb salad on top. Surround with a narrow trace of vinaigrette and with a separate ring of the reduced mushroom cooking liquid.

> The taste of the rolled oats goes perfectly with that of the hazelnut oil, and the girolles add a woodland note. Do not use too much of the hazelnut oil as it has a very strong taste.

To serve 4

For the oat cakes
600 ml (generous 1 pint) milk
160 g (5½–6 oz) butter
160 g (5½–6 oz) rolled porridge oats (not the instant variety)
6 eggs
salt, freshly ground pepper

For the braised girolle mushrooms
240 g (½ lb) fresh girolle mushrooms
40 g (1½ oz) butter
1 tbsp hazelnut oil
salt, freshly ground pepper

For the herb salad
100 g (3½ oz) young, tender herbs (chervil, flat-leaved parsley, chives, rocket)
½ tbsp sherry vinegar
2 tbsp hazelnut oil
salt, freshly ground pepper

Vegetarian foods and vegetables

Girolle mushrooms, cream of artichokes, artichoke crisps and walnut oil

For the cream of Jerusalem
artichokes and crisps
500 g (1–1¼ lb) Jerusalem
artichokes
1 mild white onion
50 g (2 oz) unsalted butter
1 litre (1¾ pints) chicken
stock
250 ml (9 fl oz) single
(pouring) cream
1 litre (1¾ pints) oil for frying
salt, freshly ground white
pepper

For the puree of flat-
leaved parsley
1 large bunch flat-leaved
parsley
½ medium-sized, mild white
onion
100 ml (3½ fl oz) crème
fraîche
salt, freshly ground white
pepper

For the sautéed girolle
mushrooms
350 g (¾ lb) fresh girolle
mushrooms
50 g (2 oz) unsalted butter
salt, freshly ground pepper

For the dressing
2 tbsps walnut oil

Cream of Jerusalem artichokes

Peel the artichokes with a potato peeler. Rinse them and blot dry. Reserve 2 of the most regular-shaped artichokes; cut the rest into fairly large pieces. Peel the onion and slice into thin rings.

Heat the butter in a heavy-bottomed saucepan, add the onion and cook gently until tender but not browned at all. Add the artichokes and the chicken stock; boil gently for approximately 30 minutes, or until the artichokes are very tender. Once they are done, add the cream, bring back to boiling point and then liquidize in the blender or food processor until smooth. Add salt and pepper to taste.

Jerusalem artichoke crisps

Cut the 2 remaining artichokes lengthwise into very thin slices (use a mandoline cutter or a very sharp knife) and deep-fry in the very hot oil (160 °C) until they are golden brown and crisp. Remove from the oil and drain on paper towels, sprinkle with salt and keep hot, uncovered.

Puree of flat-leaved parsley

Use only the leaves of the parsley (removing all the stalks) and rinse. To 'set' the colour, blanch in a saucepan of boiling salted water, allowing 30 g (scant 2 tbsps or 1 oz) salt for each 1 litre (1¾ pints) water, then drain and immediately rinse under the cold tap; blot dry in a clean cloth. Cut the onion into small dice. Heat the crème fraîche and the onion in an uncovered saucepan and simmer until reduced and thickened considerably. Process the reduced crème fraîche, the onion and the blanched parsley leaves in the blender or food processor until very smooth; season with salt and pepper.

Sautéed girolle mushrooms

Clean and trim the girolles, rinse briefly under the cold tap, drain well. Heat the butter in a frying pan and sauté the girolles until they are lightly browned (about 10 minutes). Season with salt and pepper to taste.

Assembling the dish

On each of 4 heated shallow soup plates or fairly deep dishes, place one-quarter of the girolles mixture; in the centre of this place a spoonful of the parsley puree, garnish with artichoke crisps and surround with a very thin ribbon of walnut oil. Use a hand-held electric beater to combine the remaining walnut oil with the cream of Jerusalem artichoke soup and serve very hot, in separate bowls.

This spectrum of autumn colours and tastes is enhanced by the vivid green of the parsley. Choose small, very fresh girolles that will all take the same amount of time to cook; they should still have a little 'bite' to them when done.

Fruits and vegetables of the Languedoc

We created a 'vegetarian and vegetable' menu for the Compagnie des Comptoirs, not in response to current fashion, but because we are passionate about the vegetables of the Languedoc-Roussillon region in southern France. The lively, light and versatile nature of these specialities is a secret long shared by the Mediterranean countries. In our part of the world, vegetables have always been valued for themselves and not limited to the role of a mere culinary foil. Far from being the gastronomic self-denial frequently associated with vegetarian cooking, our approach focuses on whole-hearted enjoyment. How could it be otherwise with so many wonderful plants, herbs and fruits just there for the picking?

In the Languedoc, local produce is all about colours, flavours and scents. This area epitomizes the south of France, especially westward, towards Perpignan and Roussillon, the Catalan part of the

The wonderful vegetables of southern France benefit from the bright light of Languedoc, flourishing in the heat and sun.
Above: *all is ready for lunch on the beach, in the shaded and peaceful surroundings of the Compagnie des Comptoir's Effet Mer restaurant.*
Left: *the reed beds of La Petite Camargue in the Gard.*

country, beyond the River Aude and its wetlands. With the rest of France to the east, Spain to the west, the mountainous Cevennes to the north and the Mediterranean to the south, we can choose from the foods produced in the wooded and rocky uplands, such as wild mushrooms and truffles; goats' or ewes' milk cheeses from the limestone plateaux of the Causses and the Montagne Noire (Black Mountain) area; the fruits of the sea; and all that flourishes on our sandy plains and in our orchards and vegetable plots. We tend our vegetables as if they were jewels.

Treasures from our soil

What other vegetable/fruit embodies the pleasure of living in the Mediterranean region as well as the tomato, with its insatiable appetite for sunlight? Its refreshing sweetness is balm after the heat of the sun. A friend, Roger Maelstaff, is the prince of tomato growers. He cultivates a dozen or so varieties at Pouzols, in the Minervois area, among them the Spanish Moya, enormous and fleshy, one of which is enough for a salad for two; the Andine; the Ananas (or so-called 'pineapple' tomato); the ox-heart or beef tomato; the evergreen… We cannot resist the pleasure of using them raw, in sorbets, in granitas, jellied, as gaspacho, slow baked in the oven… When we need a meal of nature's fast food, nothing compares with a thickly sliced ripe, red Moya tomato, simply sprinkled

with olive oil and a small amount of good quality, coarse salt. From the number of recipes we have created using tomatoes, it is obvious how much we love them.

The phrase 'vegetables from the South' also calls to mind tender broad beans, asparagus from Mauguio, the most tender baby artichokes, bulbs of fennel, aubergines and sweet peppers. Then there are the salads and herbs with their distinctive full-bodied, aromatic and sometimes peppery taste. Rocket is one such, said to be hot enough to waken the dead. Basil, chervil and the first young shoots of spinach may also be found throughout the region, whilst certain vegetables are the pride of a particular village, such as the black turnips of Pardailhan, grown only on the chalk and slate plateau of Haut-Languedoc. Official recognition in the form of an 'appellation d'origine controlée' for this exceptional root vegetable, with its sweetly aromatic and complex taste, is long overdue. The small town of Lézignan-la-Cèbe derives its name from the mild onions (known as cèbes) renowned there since the seventeenth century. They must be eaten while still fresh. The white onions from Citou (Aude), Toulouges (eastern Pyrenees) and those grown in the Cevennes are less perishable and are therefore to be found outside the Languedoc region – and outside France.

The scented fruits of the South

Which fruits should we choose as the most redolently evocative of our region? The first to spring to mind is the apricot. This golden globe with its intoxicating scent and flavour symbolizes the Languedoc-Roussillon, whether it is presented raw, or as jam, or preserved in brandy… We love to couple it with almonds and with orgeat, for a typically southern marriage. Hidden in the soil of our hinterland there is another perfumed 'fruit': the truffle, a black treasure which is traded in the markets of Uzès, Anduze and Bagnols-sur-Cèze during the winter months and accounts for approximately 15 per cent of the truffle crop in France. Of all Languedoc's fruits, however, the crown must go to the olive! The green *lucques*, the *picholine* pickling olive, the black olives used for making tapenade, and the *negrette* and *verdale* varieties that yield such precious olive oil – from our childhood, the fragrance of olive oil has surrounded us. We use it without thinking, as the air that we breathe, and its pure taste never palls. Whether as seasoning or dressing, combining different flavours or enhancing the simplest dishes, it is fundamental: a golden thread running through our cuisine.

New season's asparagus: cooked à la plancha, raw in a salad, citrus fruits and tomato salsa

Clean the asparagus and peel the lower parts of the stem with a potato peeler or special asparagus peeler, taking care not to damage their tips.

For the citrus vinaigrette
Peel the orange, pomelo and lemon with a very sharp, pointed serrated knife, removing all the pith. Extract the segments carefully from their thin, white membranes. Cut the segments into fairly small dice, add the olive oil and the diced slow-baked tomato, and season with salt and freshly ground pepper. Set aside.

For the asparagus
Heat a griddle or very wide, heavy frying pan, having first brushed the surface with oil; spread 24 asparagus spears out in a single layer and roast over a gentle heat, turning frequently until tender but still crisp. Season with salt and pepper and set aside. Slice the remaining 6 raw asparagus spears lengthwise into very thin strips, using a mandoline or very sharp knife; sprinkle with lemon juice, salt, pepper and olive oil.

To serve
Finish the preparation of the citrus vinaigrette by stirring in the coarsely snipped coriander leaves. Arrange 6 roasted asparagus spears in the centre of each plate.
Place one-quarter of the raw, dressed spears on top of each serving of roasted asparagus and surround with the citrus vinaigrette. Decorate each portion with one or two Parmesan shavings.

> Asparagus is one of our favourite vegetables and here it is prepared in two different ways for the same dish. The asparagus grown at Mauguio, near Montpellier, is renowned for its quality. Citrus fruit is the perfect complement to bring out the fresh, agreeably sharp, springtime flavour of new season's asparagus. It is unusual to grill or sear vegetables: once you try it, you will be a convert.

Fresh goat's cheeses, roast apricots, spicy layered pastry slices, caramelized Banyuls wine

4 fresh, mild, white goat's
cheeses, weighing
approximately 100–125 g
(3½–4 oz) each
700 ml (1¼ pints) Banyuls
wine (natural sweet, French
fortified white wine)
olive oil

Spicy layered pastry
500 g (1 lb) filo pastry (see
note at end of recipe)
100 g (3½ oz) butter, melted
selection of white, black,
green and pink peppercorns
(see method)
icing sugar

Roast apricots
6 naturally ripened, best
quality apricots
salt, freshly ground pepper

Boil the Banyuls wine in an uncovered saucepan until it has reduced to a syrupy consistency: it is ready when it lightly coats the bottom of the saucepan when the pan is tipped to one side. If reduced excessively, the syrup will be bitter.

Preheat the oven to 180 °C (gas mark 6). Rinse the apricots, cut them in half, remove their stones and cut into quarters. Set aside.

Spicy layered pastry

Lightly grease a baking sheet with butter and spread a sheet of filo out on it. Brush all over the surface with melted butter. Use a pepper mill filled with a selection of the peppercorns to sprinkle lightly with freshly ground pepper mixture. Cover with another sheet of filo, brush this in turn with butter and sprinkle again with pepper mixture. Repeat until you have 4 layers of filo pastry sheets, sprinkling the last sheet with a light dusting of sifted icing sugar. Use a large, sharp knife to cut the layered filo into rectangles measuring 5 cm x 10 cm (2 in x 4 in). Place a second baking sheet, non-stick side downwards, on top of the filo and bake in the oven for 15 minutes. Keep hot.

Roasted apricots

Heat a griddle or a very large, heavy frying pan. Pour in 2 tbsps olive oil and 'roast' the apricot quarters, allowing them to colour on both sides. Season to taste.

To serve

Place a goat's cheese, cut in half, on each plate and arrange a few quarters of roast apricot to one side. Drizzle a thin stream of the caramelized wine over the fruit. Garnish with a spicy pastry and finish with a trickle of olive oil.

Filo pastry is widely available now, wherever Greek or Middle-Eastern foods are sold. It should not be confused with brick, another Middle-Eastern pastry, which is sold lightly cooked and is thicker. Filo is paper thin and very smooth. Cover the filo that is waiting to be used with a damp cloth as it dries out very quickly. This spicy, crunchy layered pastry is a wonderful accompaniment to the creamy texture of the fresh white goat's cheese: one of the best is Pélardon from the Cevennes, a mountainous district of south-western France.

Pan-roasted slices of water melon, soy and caramelized balsamic vinegar sauce, cream cheese shake

Soy and caramelized balsamic vinegar sauce

Mix the balsamic vinegar with the sugar in a saucepan and cook until reduced by half; add the soy sauce and set aside at room temperature.

Pan-roasted water melon slices

Cut 4 rectangular slices out of the water melon, measuring approximately 10 cm x 4 cm (4 in x 1½ in). Dip these in the soy sauce. Melt the sugar over a moderate heat in a non-stick saucepan; increase the heat and 'pan-roast' the water melon slices briefly on both sides.

Cream cheese shake

Put the cheeses in a food processor or large blender; pour in the milk and olive oil. Season with salt and pepper and add the ice cubes; process at maximum speed, blending these ingredients thoroughly before pouring into chilled glasses.

To serve

Place a water melon rectangle on each plate. Surround with equal quantities of the soy and balsamic caramel sauce. Serve with the cream cheese shake.

This very simple recipe, with its unusual preparation of the water melon, will surprise and delight your guests. The Kikkoman brand of soy sauce, with its full-bodied yet delicate flavour, is well suited to all these Far-Eastern dishes.

To serve 4

For the soy and caramelized balsamic vinegar sauce
200 ml (7 fl oz) balsamic vinegar
40 g (1½ oz) caster sugar
1 tbsp Kikkoman soy sauce (see note at end of method)

For the pan-roasted water melon slices
½ water melon
3 tbsps Kikkoman soy sauce (see note at end of method)
50 g (2 oz) caster sugar

For the cream cheese shake
4 small, fresh white cow's milk cheeses (Carré type)
200 ml (7 fl oz) milk, chilled
1 tbsp olive oil
salt, freshly ground white pepper
2 ice cubes

Chilled avocado smoothie with tomato and fresh chilli salsa

To serve 4

For the avocado smoothie
4 ripe avocados
500 ml (18 fl oz) fresh chicken
stock, chilled
juice of 1 lemon
olive oil
1 small de-seeded chilli
pepper, crushed
salt, freshly ground pepper

**For the lemon-flavoured
olive oil ice cubes**
3 tbsps olive oil
1 tbsp lemon juice
salt

To garnish
1 large, ripe, flavoursome
tomato
small bunch coriander
best quality coarse salt (*fleur
de sel* or Maldon), freshly
ground pepper
4 *grissini* Italian breadsticks
(see note at end of recipe)

Avocado smoothie
Peel the avocados and remove their stones. Place them in the bowl of a food processor or a blender with the chicken stock, lemon juice, a very little olive oil, and salt and pepper to taste. Process until very smooth; if the mixture is too thick, add a plain ice cube. Add as much (or as little) as you like of the crumbled dried chilli (having first removed and discarded the seeds) and finish processing.

Lemon-flavoured olive oil ice cubes
Beat the olive oil with the lemon juice and the salt. Fill 4 sections of an ice cube tray with small, water-tight divisions and place in the freezer.

To serve
Peel the tomato after blanching it briefly in boiling water, remove the seeds and cut into very small dice. Take the coriander leaves off their stalks.

Select 4 large glasses. In each of these place a small quantity of the diced tomato, followed by a few coriander leaves. Add 1 lemon-flavoured ice cube, sprinkle with coarse salt and freshly ground pepper. Place a breadstick in the glass. Serve the chilled avocado smoothie in a glass carafe and hand round, for each person to pour some into their own glass.

The creamiest avocados are the Haas type, with their rather dark, granular skins; use these if they are available. Italian *grissini* are widely sold; buy the smallest and thinnest you can find for this recipe.

Puree of artichokes, slivers of raw baby artichokes, orange ice lollies, olive oil

1 lemon (to stop the
artichokes discolouring)

For the artichoke puree
14 very young violet
artichokes
2 tbsps olive oil
30 g (1 oz) fat from raw, cured
ham (Bayonne, Serrano,
Denhay), very finely chopped
1 small, mild white onion or
large spring onion, finely
chopped
100 ml (3½ fl oz) fresh
chicken stock
juice of 1 lemon

**For the sliced baby
artichokes**
2 very young violet artichokes
juice of 1 lemon
100 ml (3½ fl oz) olive oil
1 large, ripe skinned tomato,
de-seeded and diced
small bunch of chives
salt, freshly ground pepper

For the orange ice lollies
juice of 2 oranges
juice of ½ lemon
100 ml (3½ fl oz) olive oil
salt, freshly ground pepper
16 thin wooden skewers or
bamboo satay sticks

Prepare all the artichokes: 14 for the puree and 2 to be served raw.
Taking one artichoke at a time, remove the lower, outer leaves to expose the base using a very sharp, small paring knife; cut off most of the stalk, leaving only a short length of stalk attached. Cut off most of the leaves one by one, working round the artichoke and 'turning' it as you do so. When done, cut off the tips of the remaining leaves. Rub all the exposed, cut surfaces with lemon juice. As each artichoke is prepared, add it to a large bowl of cold water, acidulated with lemon juice.

Orange ice lollies

Place all the ingredients in a bowl and blend with a hand-held electric mixer. Season to taste. Pour into 16 watertight sections of an ice cube tray and place in the deep freeze. After 1 hour, push a wooden skewer or satay stick deep into the centre of each cube and return to the freezer.

Puree of artichokes

Heat 1 tbsp olive oil with the ham fat. Cook gently for a few minutes, add the onion and continue cooking until soft but do not brown at all. Add the 14 well-drained, prepared artichoke hearts and stir for a few minutes. Sprinkle with all the chicken stock and simmer gently until the artichoke hearts are tender (approximately 20 minutes).
Place the artichokes and all their cooking juices in a food processor or blender and add the remaining olive oil and the lemon juice; process until very smooth; chill in the refrigerator.

Sliced raw artichokes

Begin by making the salsa or dressing for these: mix the lemon juice with the olive oil, tomato, chopped chives, salt and freshly ground pepper. Use a mandoline cutter or a very sharp knife to cut the remaining 2 artichokes lengthwise into very thin slices and add to the dressing immediately to prevent them discolouring. Mix well to coat thoroughly; adjust the seasoning to taste.

To serve

Use long, narrow oval hors d'oeuvre dishes if possible: spaced out along each dish, place 4 tbsps of the puree. Place an orange ice lolly on top of each mound of puree and then distribute the raw artichoke slices carefully on top, with their stalks uppermost. Garnish with the tomato salsa and more chopped chives. Serve at once.

The process of 'turning' or paring the artichokes is fiddly but worth it as it reveals the most tender and intensely flavoured part of the violet or 'poivrade' artichoke, which flourishes in sunny climates. Always rub lemon juice immediately over cut surfaces to prevent discolouration. Fat from the best quality raw, cured ham imparts a very special flavour that adds a subtle dimension to the dish.

Tomato tartare, Moya ice cubes, toasted-almond milk

For the tomato tartare
4 naturally ripened, deep red, flavoursome tomatoes
bunch of chives

For the tomato granita (or ice cubes)
250 (9 oz) deep red tomato flesh (see note at end of method)
80 ml (3 fl oz) tomato juice
10 g (scant 1 tbsp) thick tomato puree (paste)
1 tbsp olive oil
juice of ½ lemon
pinch of caster sugar
salt, freshly ground pepper

For the toasted-almond milk
200 g (7 oz) whole, blanched, skinned almonds
250 ml (9 fl oz) milk
250 ml (9 fl oz) crème fraîche
2 tbsps almond oil
salt, freshly ground white pepper

To serve
olive oil
small bunch of fresh basil
salt, freshly ground pepper

Preheat the oven to 180 °C (gas mark 6).

For the tomato tartare

Blanch the tomatoes briefly in boiling water and then skin them. Remove all their seeds and cut the flesh into small dice. Set aside. Snip the chives into very short lengths and chill separately.

Tomato granita

Place the 250 g (9 oz) of tomato flesh, cut into large pieces, into the bowl of the food processor; add the tomato juice, the tomato puree, olive oil, lemon juice, sugar, salt and pepper. Process at very high speed, then taste and add more seasoning if necessary. Rub this puree through a sieve (a stainless-steel conical chinois if you have one) and then pour the puree into ice cube trays, with or without the divisions in place. Place in the freezer.

Toasted-almond milk

Spread the almonds out on a baking sheet and toast them in the oven for about 5–7 minutes. Take them out of the oven when they start to turn a pale golden-brown colour. Bring the milk and the crème fraîche to the boil together in a large saucepan. Add the almonds, turn off the heat and leave to stand for 20 minutes to flavour the creamy milk. Add the almond oil and blend this with the almonds and milk, using a hand-held electric blender. Add salt and pepper to taste and leave to cool. Chill slightly if wished.

To serve

Season the tomato tartare with salt and pepper, add the chives.

Using individual bowls or deep soup plates, place 1 tbsp of the tomato tartare in the bottom of each. Pour some of the chilled almond milk into each bowl. Break up the frozen tomato mixture or ice cubes with the prongs of a fork and place 1 tbsp on top of each spoonful of tomato tartare. Add a trickle of olive oil and decorate with a sprig of basil.

> In this recipe tomatoes are given two treatments, both light and refreshing, to bring out the wonderful flavour of naturally sun-ripened tomatoes when they are in season.
> Some rare varieties (cultivated by our friend Roger Maelstaff) such as Moya, a large and very flavoursome Spanish tomato, are used in the Company des Comptoirs' restaurants.

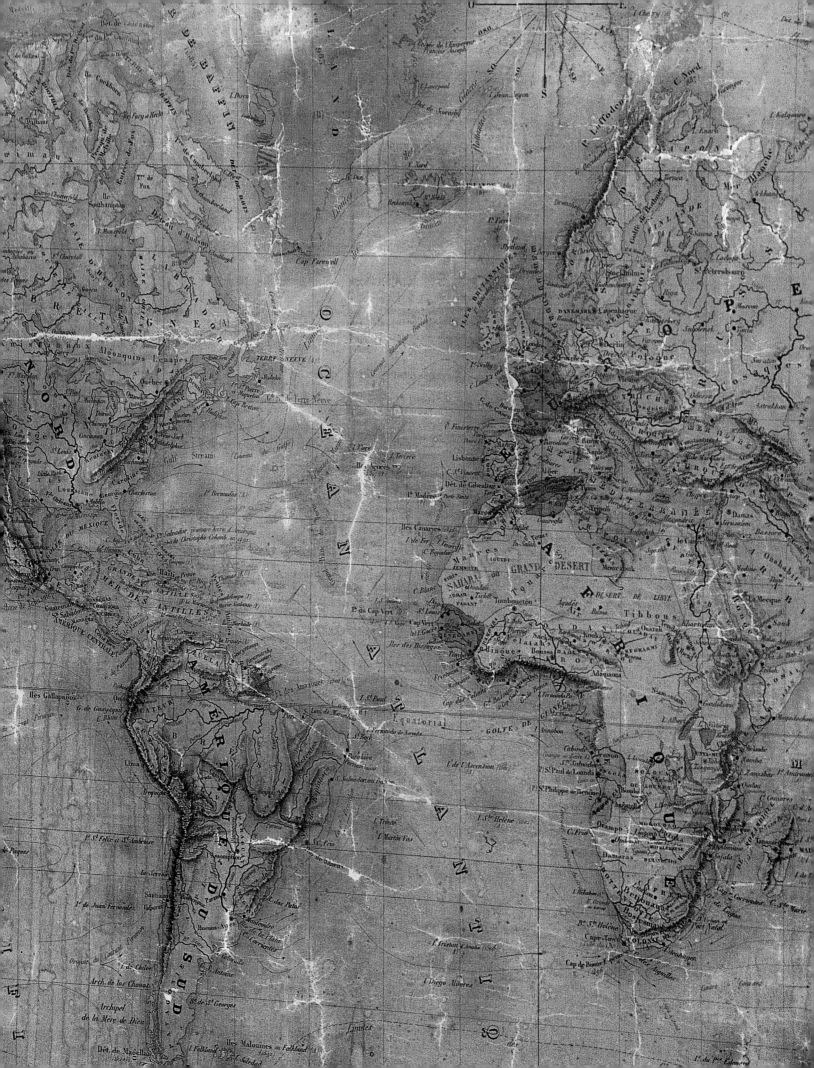

Fruits and vegetables from other lands

Long before 'fusion cooking' became fashionable, it was an everyday practice in these parts. Professor Jean-Robert Pitte's provocative dictum, 'cassoulet is an American dish', springs to mind. As it happens, only the pork and duck in the recipe are native to this region, the beans and the tomatoes both coming from the New World, yet this dish epitomizes our local culinary traditions.

This is no isolated phenomenon: it is a recurrent feature of all cooking. Without the ceaseless migration of ingredients and tastes facilitated by commercial contacts, chance meetings and conquests, each country would be restricted to its own, very monotonous, diet.

The great majority of the fruit and vegetables we most frequently use and enjoy originated in the natural plant nurseries of the New World and Central Asia. Sometimes we find ourselves wondering what our food would be like had the Americas never been discovered, while many of our familiar

Above: *a warehouse on the docks in the Port du Commerce in Marseilles, its windows gilded by the setting sun, evokes the thought of other sunsets, just as flamboyant, far away across the world.*
Left: *one of the antique maps which, together with old books about long-ago journeys and colonial prints, help create the atmosphere of travel and adventure at the Compagnie des Comptoirs.*

fruits and oleaginous plants, such as almonds, apricots, peaches, cherries, walnuts, pistachios, citrus fruits, have reached us from Asia. Products, dishes and culinary styles migrate and, like all migrants, bring with them contributions that influence each other and intermingle. Spices, aromatics, vegetables and fruits seem always to be on the move. Some of these imports have become so popular and widely accepted that we forget how far they have travelled from their original habitats. We assume that they have appeared on our tables since time immemorial.

Peripatetic plants

Until the early twentieth century, the orange, in common with other citrus fruits, was still a rare treat and was often the only gift that children of impecunious families could expect at Christmas. Cultivated strawberries reached us only relatively recently, being brought back from Chile during the seventeenth century, although long before that the Gauls and Romans greatly enjoyed small, wild, native strawberries. The Spanish conquistadores introduced the tomato from Peru but it was

Vegetarian foods and vegetables

Above, left: *small, hot peppers, both green and red, are always in plentiful supply in Asian food stores.*
Above, right: *Chinese carp in one of the pools at the Compagnie des Comptoirs.*

shunned for a long time because of its sinister reputation; in common with other plants belonging to the solanaceae family (of which tobacco, deadly nightshade and datura are among the poisonous members) it was believed to be toxic, if not devilish. Once it was adopted by Mediterranean cooks, however, it caused so much excitement and inspired so many delicious recipes that we can only assume that it filled a culinary gap! It is one of the ironies of such migrations of foodstuffs that this native of the Andes had to wait until the nineteenth century before it was accepted in North America. Nowadays, it is as difficult to imagine Italian cooking without tomatoes as the United States without tomato ketchup! The aubergine is known to have existed four thousand years ago in East Asia, being introduced to Europe during the Middle Ages by the Muslim population of Andalusia. In the South of France, all that was missing for the invention of ratatouille was the cour-gette: when marrows and sweet peppers arrived in their turn from the New World, this tasty selec-tion of sun-loving vegetables was complete.

Peppers, pimentos and chillis are travellers par excellence. They have spread all over the world from Central America, where they were first discovered. In Africa and Asia, many wild and cultivated vari-eties have developed with the result that the capsicum has become the most varied genus of plants used for flavouring food. In Europe, the greatest quantities are consumed in Hungary (paprika) and throughout the Mediterranean basin.

A culinary laboratory

What all this tells us is that the Mediterranean region, which adopted a great number of vegetables and fruits long before they were accepted in northern countries, can be thought of as a sort of culinary laboratory through which the whole of Europe became accustomed to foods from far-off lands. The southerners' liking for strong tastes and aromas encouraged adventurous cooking, and the recipes of the Compagnie des Comptoirs perpetuate this process.

When we blend tomatoes with pineapple in a refreshing gaspacho soup or make the unexpected addition of sweet potatoes or sweetcorn to our blinis, we are being just as daring as our ancestors when they decided to add tomatoes or beans to a dish.

Tradition and innovation go hand in hand: our chilled avocado smoothie with tomato salsa and fresh chillis, for example, echoes the ingredients of Mexican guacamole. We use the sweet potato in both sweet and savoury dishes, just as they do on the other side of the Atlantic. As for marrows, pumpkins and squashes, each variety has its own distinctive taste and texture. We particularly love the small, bright orange pumpkin, the Japanese squash with its delicious chestnut taste, and the American variety, the butternut – whose name conjures up its buttery taste and consistency – as well as the muskmarrow. We serve pumpkin as a thick, creamy soup, but also use it to make sweet fritters for the dessert course.

Above: *a fruit vendor's display in a Malaysian market. Some tropical fruits are not exported to Europe and are gathered for local consumption only. The durian, with its unforgettable odour, is one example. Despite its smell, the flesh tastes good and the fruit is much sought after in Malaysia and in Hong Kong.*

Vegetarian foods and vegetables∫

Multicoloured tomato salad made à la Roger, green tomato sorbet

For the green tomato sorbet

500 g (1–1¼ lb) small green tomatoes (evergreen, see note at end of method)

100 ml (3½ fl oz) sugar syrup made with 100 ml (3½ fl oz) water and 100g (3½ oz) sugar

For the Parmesan brick pastry rectangles

1 sheet of *brick* (North-African thin pastry)

1 egg yolk

40 g (1½ oz) freshly and finely grated Parmesan cheese

For the sliced tomato salad

1 large yellow tomato (Ananas variety if available)

4 orange tomatoes (Andine variety if available)

2 very large bright red tomatoes (Moya, if available)

To serve

pinch of caster sugar

best coarse salt (French *fleur de sel* or Maldon)

freshly grated pepper

olive oil

Green tomato sorbet

Rinse the green tomatoes and wipe them dry; cut them into large pieces and process them with the sugar syrup until the mixture is smooth. Use a sorbetière if you have one, or an ice-cream maker, to quick-freeze the mixture and then transfer to the freezer.

Parmesan brick pastry

Preheat the oven to 180 °C (gas mark 6). Cut the sheet of brick pastry into 4 rectangles of equal size. Brush the surface of these all over with the lightly beaten egg yolk and sprinkle evenly with freshly and finely grated Parmesan cheese. Bake them on a baking sheet for 7–10 minutes in the oven, or until they have started to brown. Remove from the oven. Transfer to a cake rack and leave to cool.

Multicoloured tomato salad

Wash the tomatoes and remove their skins; if they are very ripe these may be easy to peel off; running the blade of a knife gently, at an angle, all over the surface will help loosen the skin. If necessary blanch in boiling water for a few seconds, plunge into cold water and then peel. Remove their stalks and any hard part beneath the stalk. Slice from top to bottom into neat, thick slices.

To serve

Arrange the tomato slices, slightly overlapping, on 4 plates, alternating the colours. Sprinkle with sugar, with the special salt and with freshly ground pepper, and then drizzle a little olive oil over them.

Use a stainless steel tablespoon to scoop out 4 egg-shaped 'quenelles' of green tomato sorbet and place one in the centre of each plate. Add a Parmesan pastry rectangle to each plate and serve.

> Our friend Roger and the unusual varieties of tomatoes he cultivates (see previous page) have inspired this sensual and vividly coloured version of the classic tomato salad. If you cannot get hold of these rare tomatoes, look for some unusual ones in your local shops, choosing different colours (yellow, for instance) as well as differently shaped ones: Roma, Marmande, beef and Andean tomatoes… Ideally, they should be home grown and fresh picked from your garden, grow-bag or window box. When it comes to the sorbet, do not use under-ripe green tomatoes; evergreen, as the name suggests, remain green when fully ripe. Use Roma or Olivette tomatoes if evergreen are unavailable.

Gaspacho jelly, curried courgette caviar, cucumber crunch

Gaspacho

Blanch, peel, trim and de-seed the tomatoes. Place all the ingredients with the exception of the gelatine in the blender or food processor and process. Taste and add more seasoning if wished; strain through a fine mesh, non-metallic sieve, or stainless steel conical chinois if you have one.

You will need approximately 6 leaves of gelatine (or 1½ sachets powdered gelatine) for each 1 litre (1¾ pints) of gaspacho. As the quantities given for this recipe usually yield approximately 1½ litres (2½ pints) of gaspacho, 8 or 9 leaves (2 sachets if powdered) should be enough. Soak the leaves in cold water to soften. Warm a little water gently in a saucepan, remove it from the heat and add the gelatine leaves. Leave them to dissolve completely, stirring occasionally. If you choose to use powdered gelatine, carrageen or agar-agar, follow the manufacturer's instructions on the packet. Add the gelling agent to the gaspacho, stirring well as you do so. Chill in the refrigerator for approximately 6 hours.

Courgette caviar

Bring plenty of salted water to the boil in a large saucepan. Wash the courgettes, trim off their ends and slice them lengthwise. Cut away or scoop out the centre section which is softer and contains the seeds, leaving only the firmer parts and the skin. Cook the strips of courgette in the boiling water until just tender but still firm; drain and rinse well under the cold tap. Drain in a colander; squeeze dry very gently with a clean cloth. Heat the crème fraîche over a gentle heat, uncovered, until it has reduced and thickened considerably. Place the courgette strips, the curry powder, olive oil and crème fraiche in the food processor or blender and process until very smooth. Add salt and pepper to taste. Chill in the refrigerator.

Cucumber crunch

Peel the cucumber and dice it. Add the finely snipped chives, the diced tomato, olive oil and lemon juice; season with salt and pepper to taste.

To serve

Place 2 tablespoons of gaspacho jelly in the bottom of 4 small, deep glass dishes or coupes, cover with cucumber crunch. Spoon in the courgette caviar and finish with a level teaspoon of natural yoghurt. Sprinkle with a pinch of special salt and a twist of pepper from the peppermill. Trickle a little olive oil on top, followed by a pinch of curry powder.

> We make this recipe with our favourite tomato grower's produce, but you can substitute any other varieties, provided they are really ripe, full flavoured and fragrant. If you want to embellish the dish further, cut slivers of young courgettes and deep-fry these until crisp; use them to decorate this refreshing starter: the crispiness will complement the summery vegetables.

Gaspacho jelly

1.2 kg (2½–2¾ lb) ripe, deep red tomatoes
800 ml (1 pint 8 fl oz) tomato juice
1 tsp tomato puree (paste)
100 ml (3½ fl oz) olive oil
pinch of caster sugar
juice of 1 lemon
salt, freshly ground pepper
8 or 9 leaves of gelatine (see method for alternatives)

For the courgette caviar

6 medium-sized courgettes
100 ml (3½ fl oz) crème fraîche
generous pinch of mild or medium curry powder
3 tbsps olive oil
salt, freshly ground pepper

For the cucumber crunch

1 cucumber
small bunch of chives
1 very red, ripe tomato (see recipe on p. 48), de-seeded, diced
1 tbsp olive oil
a squeeze of lemon juice
salt, freshly ground pepper

To serve

1 small pot natural yoghurt
olive oil
mild or medium curry powder
best quality coarse salt (*fleur de sel*, Maldon), freshly ground pepper

vegetarian first courses

49

Vegetarian foods and vegetables

Grilled vine tomatoes, mozzarella, lettuce heart, balsamic caramel dressing

4 bunches or sprays of cherry
vine tomatoes (approximately
12 tomatoes on each)
300 ml (10½–11 fl oz)
balsamic vinegar
juice of 1 lemon
olive oil
salt, freshly ground pepper

To serve

1 or 2 very fresh, large, pale-
green lettuce hearts
250 g (9 oz) buffalo milk
mozzarella cheese(s)
fresh chervil for decoration
olive oil
best coarse salt (Maldon,
French *fleur de sel*)

Heat the balsamic vinegar and cook, uncovered, over a gentle heat until it acquires a syrupy consistency. Check by tilting the saucepan to one side: if the syrup leaves a light coating on the bottom of the pan, it is ready. Watch carefully during the later stages of the reduction as it can burn easily! Rinse the lettuce leaves and dry with paper towels. Make a vinaigrette with the lemon juice, 2 tbsps olive oil, salt and pepper. Heat a little olive oil in a frying pan, place the sprays of tomatoes in the pan and cook over a gentle heat.

To serve
Slice the mozzarella cheese(s) thickly and arrange on 4 plates, adding the lettuce leaves tossed in the lemon vinaigrette and one spray of vine tomatoes per portion. Sprinkle with a little olive oil, the balsamic caramel dressing and some special coarse salt. Decorate with sprigs of chervil.

A delicious cocktail of Italian tastes, subtly enhanced by the caramelized balsamic vinegar. The best lettuce to use for this recipe is the round or cabbage lettuce.

Vegetarian foods and vegetables

Quick tomato and pineapple gaspacho, lime and soy granita

To serve 4

For the lime and soy
granita
150 g (5 oz) caster sugar
100 ml (3½ fl oz) light soy
sauce
juice of 3 limes
100 ml (3½ fl oz) water

For the tomato and
pineapple gaspacho
1 kg (2¼ lb) deep red, ripe
tomatoes
1 small ripe pineapple
pinch of caster sugar
100 ml (3½ fl oz) olive oil
salt, freshly ground pepper

To serve
1 ripe, very red tomato (see
preparation method on p. 48),
de-seeded
small bunch chives
olive oil

Lime and soy granita

The day before you plan to serve this dish, make a syrup with the sugar and 250 ml (9 fl oz) water. Mix the soy sauce, lime juice and the extra water with the finished, cooled syrup in a freezer-proof, non-metallic or plastic bowl and place in the freezer for at least 12 hours.

Tomato and pineapple gaspacho

Blanch and skin the tomatoes; cut them into large pieces, discarding the seeds and any tough parts. Peel the pineapple, remove the hard central section and cut the flesh into cubes. Place the tomatoes, three-quarters of the pineapple flesh, a pinch of sugar and the olive oil in the bowl of a food processor and reduce to a smooth puree. Season with salt and pepper to taste. Chill in the refrigerator.

To serve

Cut the remaining pineapple flesh and the tomato into very small dice. Mix with the finely snipped or chopped chives. Chill in the refrigerator.

Using deep soup plates or shallow bowls, place 1–2 tablespoons of the chilled tomato, pineapple and chive mixture in each. Use the prongs of a fork to break up the lemon-soy sorbet and shape the resulting granita into 4 oval 'quenelles' using 2 tablespoons; place each one, as soon as it has been shaped, on top of the tomato, pineapple and chive mixture. Surround with the chilled gaspacho and finish with a trickle of olive oil.

> You have probably never tried the combination of tomato and pineapple: you will enjoy this harmonious blend of summer tastes, a mixture of aromatic sweetness, freshness and sharpness. Every component of this recipe must be served while still very cold.

Vegetarian foods and vegetables

Pasta with broccoli, rocket pesto and grilled Provolone cheese

To serve 4

Rocket pesto

Put the rocket, peeled garlic cloves and the olive oil in the food processor; add a little salt and then process to a smooth paste. Mix thoroughly in a bowl with the ground almonds, the Parmesan cheese and pepper to taste.

Orecchiette pasta and broccoli

Trim and wash the broccoli; detach the floret tops and set aside. Use the upper part of the stalk and the beginnings of the 'branches' from which you have cut the florets and cut into slivers with a mandoline or a very sharp knife. Boil the broccoli florets in plenty of salted water for only a few minutes, just until they are barely tender. Rinse them immediately under the cold tap, drain and set aside.

Bring to the boil plenty of salted water with a few drops of olive oil added to it in a large saucepan. Add the pasta and cook until al dente (tender but still with a little 'bite' to them); drain at once. Heat 1 tbsp olive oil in a non-stick frying pan and fry the thinly sliced pieces of broccoli stalks briefly over a moderate heat until just tender. Season to taste.

To serve

Mix the florets and the stalks gently together, off the heat. Add to the hot pasta, with 3 tablespoons of the rocket pesto, the crème fraîche and diced tomato.

Slice the Provolone cheese; heat briefly over a high heat, turning once, in the non-stick frying pan, place on top of the pasta and broccoli and serve immediately.

This Italian-inspired dish can be served either as a first course or as a light main course. Be careful not to overcook the florets: they should be tender but firm, as should the stalks. For a stronger taste, use unmatured Pecorino, a sheep's milk cheese with the same semi-hard consistency as Provolone when it has not been allowed to age. Provolone, a pressed curd cow's milk cheese, varies from mild to fairly full flavoured, depending on maturation. Use the best, fruitiest olive oil.

For the rocket pesto

100 g (3½ oz) rocket leaves, washed and dried
5 cloves of garlic, peeled
500 ml (18 fl oz) olive oil
50 g (2 oz) ground almonds
50 g (2 oz) freshly grated Parmesan cheese
salt, freshly ground pepper

For the pasta and broccoli

200 g (7 oz) orecchiette or similar fresh short pasta
150 g (5 oz) broccoli
olive oil
salt, freshly ground pepper

To serve

1 tbsp crème fraîche
1 skinned tomato (see recipe on p. 48), de-seeded and diced
150 g (5 oz) Provolone Italian cheese (see note at end of method)

53

Vegetarian foods and vegetables

Baby violet artichokes Italian-style, rocket salad, Parmesan shavings

Pour les tomates confites
3 ripe, deep red tomatoes
500 ml (18 fl oz) olive oil
2 pinches of caster sugar
2 pinches of salt

For the caramelized
balsamic vinegar
500 ml (18 fl oz) balsamic
vinegar

For the marinated
artichokes
12 baby violet artichokes
2 lemons (to prevent
discolouration of the
artichokes)
500 ml (18 fl oz) olive oil
100 ml (3½ fl oz) white wine
vinegar

For the basil-flavoured oil
1 large bunch fresh basil
250 ml (9 fl oz) olive oil
salt

For the rocket salad
120 g (4 oz) rocket leaves
3 tbsps olive oil
1 tbsp lemon juice
salt, freshly ground pepper

Garnish with
8 Parmesan cheese shavings

Slow-baked tomatoes (tomates confites)

Preheat the oven to 80 °C (gas mark 2–3). Make small surface slits in the tomato skins and plunge them into boiling water for 10–20 seconds (depending on how ripe they are). Immediately transfer them to a bowl of iced water (use ice cubes). Peel and quarter them, remove the inner divisions, the seeds and any hard parts, leaving just quarters or 'petals' of flesh. Cover a baking sheet with non-stick greaseproof or silicone paper; sprinkle the surface with half the olive oil and half the sugar and salt. Spread out the tomato petals in a single layer. Sprinkle with the remaining sugar, salt and oil. Slow bake the tomatoes in the oven (this method extracts a considerable amount of their moisture) for approximately 2½ hours, turning them from time to time.

Caramelized balsamic vinegar

Pour the vinegar into a saucepan and reduce over a low heat until it thickens into a syrup. Take care not to let it burn! It is ready when the syrup leaves a thin coating on the bottom of the pan when the saucepan is tilted to one side. Set aside.

Marinated artichokes

Trim or 'turn' the artichokes (see recipe on page 38 for method of preparation). When they are all done, drain off the acidulated water, blot dry and roast on a ribbed griddle or ridged dry-frying pan over a high heat, turning once: they are meant to show sear lines. Transfer the artichokes to a casserole dish and add sufficient oil and vinegar to cover them. Cook over a very low heat until the artichokes are tender but still crisp. Leave in the liquid to cool completely before serving.

Basil-flavoured oil

Place the basil leaves, removed from their stalks, in a food processor or blender, add a pinch of salt and the olive oil. Process at high speed. (This oil will keep for several days in a cool place or larder fridge.)

Rocket salad

Dress the prepared rocket with the mixture of olive oil, lemon juice, salt and pepper.

To serve

Remove the artichokes from the marinade, draining them well; arrange 3 on each plate and place the rocket salad in the centre of the plate. Surround with a ribbon of basil-flavoured oil and another of caramelized balsamic vinegar. Garnish each serving with 3 tomato 'petals' and two Parmesan cheese shavings.

These marinated artichokes keep well in the refrigerator, covered in olive oil, until you need them and can be used in other salads as an interesting extra ingredient. You can preserve the 'petals' of slow-baked tomato (tomates confites) in the same way.

Griddle-roasted pumpkin, pumpkin soup, ricotta dumplings

To serve 4

For the griddle-roasted pumpkin
1 small, whole orange-fleshed pumpkin
olive oil
best quality coarse salt
(*fleur de sel*, Maldon)

For the cream of pumpkin hot soup drink
500 g (1 lb 2 oz) pumpkin (or butternut squash)
1 mild white onion
50 g (2 oz) unsalted butter
pinch of caster sugar
1 litre (1¾ pints) chicken stock
100 g (3¾ oz) peeled, cooked, unsweetened vacuum-packed sweet chestnuts
100 ml (3¾ fl oz) single (pouring) cream
salt, freshly ground pepper

For the ricotta dumplings
100 g (3½ oz) very fresh ricotta cheese
100 g (3½ oz) coarsely crushed unsalted pistachio nuts
10 g (½ oz) coarsely crushed pine nuts (kernels)
10 g (½ oz) golden sultanas, coarsely chopped
juice of ½ lemon
olive oil
salt, freshly ground pepper

Wash the small, whole pumpkin and cut it into neat, fairly thin sections (see facing page); discard the seeds and filaments; do not peel the slices.
Blanch for 4 minutes in boiling water; drain and set aside.

Cream of pumpkin hot soup drink
Peel the 500 g (generous 1 lb) piece of pumpkin or squash and remove the seeds and filaments. Dice the flesh. Peel and cut the onion into very thin slices and cook these over a gentle heat in the butter until tender but do not allow to colour. Add the diced pumpkin flesh, the sugar, chicken stock and the chestnuts (these unsweetened cooked chestnuts are available in tins or plastic vacuum packs in many good food shops); bring to the boil and simmer until the diced pumpkin is tender. When it is cooked, add the cream, bring back to the boil; remove from the heat immediately. Blend or process until smooth; season to taste and keep hot.

Ricotta cheese dumplings
Mix all the ingredients together, beating well to incorporate plenty of air.

Griddle-roasted pumpkin
Cook the pumpkin slices on a lightly oiled griddle (or use a very large, heavy frying pan) until tender, allowing them to brown well on both sides; sprinkle with best quality coarse salt.

To serve
Place 2 or 3 slices of roasted pumpkin in the centre of 4 individual plates; shape the ricotta mixture into 4 oval dumplings (see facing page) using 2 tablespoons and place each one across the centre of the pumpkin slices; surround with a trickle of oil. Serve the cream of pumpkin soup very hot, in pre-heated glasses, and sprinkle a few drops of the best quality olive oil on the top of each serving.

> Pumpkin is a member of the squash family and this variety originates from Japan; it is popular for its vivid orange flesh and has a taste reminiscent of sweet chestnuts. Butternut squash and muskmarrow, increasingly easy to buy, resemble it in taste and texture. Both go extremely well with chestnuts and dried vine fruits.

Sweetcorn blinis, baby spinach, prosciutto

For the slow-baked tomatoes

2 very red tomatoes

50 ml (2 fl oz) olive oil

2 pinches of salt

2 pinches of caster sugar

For the vinaigrette

juice of 1 lemon

5 tbsps olive oil

salt, freshly ground pepper

For the sweetcorn blinis

100 g (3½ oz) tinned sweetcorn kernels

125 g (4 oz) plain flour

2 eggs

12 g (scant ½ oz – 1 level tbsp) baking powder

200 ml (7 fl oz) milk

pinch of salt

leaves from a small bunch of fresh coriander, chopped

a little olive oil

To serve

1 packet baby spinach (select 60 leaves)

4 large, thin slices of *prosciutto* (see note at end of method)

Slow-baked tomatoes

Preheat the oven to 80 ºC (gas mark 2–3). Make small slits in the skin of the tomatoes and place in boiling water for 20 seconds. Transfer them without delay to a bowl of iced water, then peel and quarter them, removing the seeds and the inner divisions, leaving just the outer flesh 'petals'. Cover a baking sheet with non-stick greaseproof or silicone paper, sprinkle it with half the oil, followed by half the salt and sugar. Spread out the tomato quarters, well spaced out in a single layer and sprinkle with the remaining sugar and salt, followed by the remaining olive oil. Bake the tomatoes in the oven for approximately 2½ hours, turning them from time to time.

The vinaigrette

Mix all the ingredients and season with salt and pepper to taste.

Sweetcorn blinis

Make the batter: mix all the ingredients well (with the exception of the olive oil and the coriander); the mixture should be thicker than conventional pancake batter. Add the chopped coriander leaves and season to taste. Heat the olive oil in a wide, non-stick frying pan. Add the batter, a tablespoon at a time, and cook in the same way as drop-scones, turning once. Cook another batch of 4, so you have 2 blinis per person.

To serve

Have the baby spinach leaves ready rinsed and dried; toss them briefly in the lemon vinaigrette.

Place one blini on each plate, place a slice of *prosciutto* on this, followed by 2 tomato 'petals'. Add some baby spinach salad and top with a blini.

> Parma or San Daniele is the best quality cured Italian ham (prosciutto) and it must be thinly sliced. The use of the sweetcorn in the blinis adds a pleasing sweetness and agreeable texture.

Marinated salmon and breadsticks, artichoke hearts 'barigoule' with turmeric

For the spiced salmon
250 g (9 oz) salmon fillet
50g (2 oz) coarse salt
10g (½ oz) muscovado soft brown sugar
pinch of finely crushed black peppercorns
small bunch fresh dill leaves, chopped
12 very small, thin Italian breadsticks (*grissini*)

For the artichokes
12 baby violet artichokes
juice of 1 lemon
1 lemon, cut in half
2 tbsps olive oil
1 large spring onion
100 ml (3½ fl oz) dry white wine
1 garlic clove, crushed
1 bay leaf
sprig of thyme
5 cm (2 in) fresh turmeric root, grated (see note)
salt, freshly ground pepper

Dressing for the artichokes 'barigoule'
juice of ½ lemon
a few fresh coriander leaves
1 prepared ripe, red tomato (see p. 48), chopped
2 tbsps extra-virgin olive oil
salt, freshly ground pepper

To serve
100 g (3½ oz) mascarpone
fresh coriander
salt, freshly ground pepper

Begin by preparing the salmon: mix the salt with the sugar and pepper and rub well into the salmon filet; add the finely snipped dill. Place a small board and a weight on top of the fish and chill for 6 hours in the refrigerator.

Artichokes à la barigoule
Prepare the artichokes, using a small, very sharp knife: leave 3 cm (1–1¼ in) of the stalk attached, remove the lowest, outermost leaves and then snip off the top halves of the remaining leaves, working your way from the stalk towards the innermost leaves, leaving only the heart of the artichoke. Make sure that you end up with what looks like a bud. Cut off the tips of the innermost leaves and scoop out the 'choke' with a sharp-edged teaspoon. As you trim away parts of each artichoke, rub the cut surfaces with the lemon half; add each artichoke to a bowl of cold water acidulated with lemon juice to prevent discolouration.
 Heat the olive oil in a deep saucepan and cook the finely chopped spring onion without browning it. Add the well-drained artichokes, cut lengthwise into quarters, then the white wine, followed by the garlic, bay leaf, thyme and turmeric. Bring to the boil, adding enough water to cover the artichokes. Simmer until the artichokes are tender but still crisp, seasoning with salt and pepper. When they are done, take them out of the pan and reduce the cooking liquid by boiling, uncovered. Return the artichokes to the liquid and leave to cool.

Marinated salmon
Shortly before it is time to serve the salmon, rinse the fillet under the cold tap and blot dry with paper towels. Use a ham-cutting knife or similar very sharp knife to cut 12 very thin

horizontal slices from the salmon fillet. Wind each of them around a breadstick.

Dressing for the artichokes
Drain the artichokes through a fine-mesh sieve. Collect the liquid in a bowl and mix in the lemon, coriander leaves, chopped tomato and olive oil. Season to taste.

To serve
Mix a little salt and pepper with the mascarpone, beating briefly with a fork.
In each of 4 deep glass coupes or small bowls, place 12 artichoke quarters, sprinkle with the dressing. Use a dessert spoon to scoop out an egg-shaped 'dumpling' of mascarpone and place on top of the artichokes. Finally, top each serving with 3 salmon-wrapped breadsticks. Garnish with sprigs of coriander.

This recipe draws on the cooking of three parts of the world for its inspiration: the artichoke dish comes from the Mediterranean hinterland of France; turmeric and coriander from south-east Asia and the marinated salmon from Scandinavia. Asian greengrocers sell fresh turmeric, a slender rhizome reminiscent of fresh ginger in appearance but with bright orange flesh and orangey-grey skin. You can use 1 level dessertspoon of ground turmeric instead.

Duck brochettes, eggy-bread and giblet croutons, mixed baby-leaf salad

To serve 4

3 duck breasts
(or 6 *aiguillettes*, see method)
12 bamboo skewers or satay sticks
olive oil
salt, freshly ground pepper

For the eggy-bread and giblet paté croutons
3 tbsps port wine
1 shallot, finely chopped
3 duck livers
2 duck hearts
300 ml (10 fl oz) milk
1 large egg, lightly beaten
4 French bread slices (baguette loaf), cut on the slant
olive oil
salt, freshly ground pepper

For the mixed baby-leaf salad
1 large packet mixed baby salad leaves
3 tbsps hazelnut oil
1 tbsp sherry vinegar
salt, freshly ground pepper

Aiguillettes are long, thick slices of breast meat taken from either side of the breast bone; if you use these, cut each one lengthways in half. If using duck breasts, slice each one lengthways into 4 thick strips and thread them onto bamboo skewers.

Place the port wine and the chopped shallot in a saucepan and reduce until there is hardly any liquid left. Set aside.

Place the washed, trimmed duck livers and hearts in the food processor and process. Add the reduced port wine and shallot, a little salt and pepper; process very briefly. Transfer this mixture to a bowl and chill in the refrigerator.

Mixed baby-leaf salad
Make a vinaigrette with the hazelnut oil and sherry vinegar; season with salt and pepper. Set aside.

Eggy-bread and giblet croutons
Pour the milk into a shallow dish and beat the egg lightly in a separate dish. Spread an even amount of the giblet mixture firmly on to each bread slice to make it adhere. Dip each slice first in the milk, allow it to absorb the milk and then dip briefly in the beaten egg.

Heat a very little olive oil in a wide, non-stick frying pan; add the eggy-bread, giblet spread side downwards. Allow to fry and brown for 3–4 minutes, then turn over and brown the other side.

Cooking the duck brochettes
Pan-fry the skewered duck strips in the same wide, non-stick frying pan adding a very little more olive oil if necessary. Turn them once; the flesh should be brown on the outside but pink on the inside. Season with salt and pepper.

To serve
Toss the salad in the prepared vinaigrette. Place 3 duck brochettes on each plate, together with an eggy-bread and giblet crouton and some mixed baby-leaf salad. Serve at once, while the crouton and duck are still hot.

This unpretentious, rather rustic dish is an echo of long-ago duck shoots in the Languedoc and Cevennes, when feathered game used to be served accompanied by its giblets on slices of bread. Hazelnut oil adds an autumnal note.

Hot onion tart with tomatoes, sardines and herb salad

1 kg (2¼ lb) freshly caught
sardines, filleted, trimmed
4 deep red, ripe tomatoes
50 g (2 oz) Parmesan cheese
4 discs 10 cm (4 in) wide, cut
out of a sheet of puff pastry
salt, freshly ground pepper

For the onion compote
7 medium-sized, mild white
onions, very thinly sliced
20–25g (scant 1 oz) butter
pinch of caster sugar
salt, freshly ground pepper

**For the lemon and honey
vinaigrette**
juice of 3 lemons
50g (2 oz) clear, runny honey
250 ml (9 fl oz) olive oil
salt, freshly ground pepper

For the herb salad
a few rocket leaves
small bunch of chives,
snipped into fairly long
lengths
leaves from a small bunch of
very fresh coriander
leaves from a small bunch of
chervil

Use paper towels to blot the sardine fillets dry, wiping off any remaining scales. Make sure all visible bones have been removed. Blanch the tomatoes for a few seconds in boiling water and peel them. Use a cheese slicer or potato peeler to shave off flakes of Parmesan. Set all this aside ready for use.

Preheat the oven to 220 °C (gas mark 7–8).

Onion compote

Cook the onions in the butter until tender without allowing them to colour. Add the pinch of sugar. Cover and cook over a very low heat for 20 minutes or until very soft indeed, then remove the lid and allow any excess moisture to reduce and evaporate. Season to taste and keep hot.

Lemon and honey vinaigrette

Mix all the ingredients listed for this dressing.

Preparation and cooking of the pastry base

Use ready-made puff pastry; roll out to a thin sheet and cut out 4 discs measuring 10 cm (4 in) across; transfer these on a non-stick baking sheet. Prick all over the exposed surfaces with the prongs of a fork to prevent them rising too much as they cook and, for the same reason, place another baking sheet, non-stick side downwards, on top of the discs. Bake in the oven for 15 minutes. When they are done, take them out of the oven and turn up the oven temperature to 270 °C (gas mark 9).

Spread a generous tablespoonful of onion compote on each pastry round (you will need to reserve a small amount for assembling this dish); slice the tomatoes fairly thickly and arrange on top of the onions. Add the sardine fillets; season with salt and pepper. Top with the Parmesan shavings. Place in the hot oven for a few minutes to lightly cook the sardines and soften the cheese slightly.

To serve

While the pastries are in the oven, dress the herb salad with some of the lemon and honey vinaigrette.

Spread one-quarter of the remaining onion compote in the centre of each plate and put a pastry disc on top of it (this will stop them sliding around); garnish each tart with some of the salad. Encircle with a trace of olive oil and serve at once.

A traditional recipe from Nice, *pissaladière niçoise*, inspired us to include onions cooked in this way when creating these savoury pastries. White onions are chosen for the delicious sweet taste they develop after long, slow cooking. Return to the very hot oven for only as long as it takes to part-cook the sardines: they are so fresh all they need is to heat through and become firmer.

Home-smoked mackerel fillets, sweet potato blinis, chive-flavoured oil

For the smoked mackerel fillets
2 medium-sized very fresh mackerel
1 tbsp beech wood sawdust (see note at end of method)
best coarse salt, freshly ground pepper

For the chive-flavoured oil
1 bunch chives
100 ml (3½ fl oz) olive oil
salt

For the blinis
200 g (7 oz) sweet potatoes (orange flesh variety)
50 g (2 oz) plain flour
1 egg
3-4 tsps natural, full-fat yoghurt
olive oil
salt, freshly ground pepper

Fillet the mackerel, using tweezers to remove any remaining bones. Set aside.

Chive-flavoured oil
Put the oil, a generous pinch of salt and the rinsed, dried chives into the blender. Process until completely blended; set aside.

Blinis
Cook the sweet potatoes in plenty of boiling water. When they are very tender, peel them. Mash to a fine puree and, when lukewarm, mix in the flour and egg and season with salt and pepper. Add a little yoghurt at a time to achieve a thick pancake batter consistency. Heat a lightly oiled, non-stick frying pan and, when hot, add spoonfuls of the batter, sufficient to make only very small pancakes or mini-blinis. Brown lightly on both sides and allow 2–3 per person.

Home-smoked mackerel fillets
Sprinkle 1 tbsp of the beech sawdust into a very wide, non-stick frying pan. Place a rack on top of these to prevent the fish coming into direct contact with the beech wood shavings; arrange the fish fillets on the rack. Cover tightly and cook over a high heat for approximately 5 minutes (the smoking time will vary, depending on the thickness of the fillets).

To serve
Make an attractive arrangement on each plate, with the blinis on one side and the smoked fish in the middle, surrounded by a thin ribbon of chive dressing. Sprinkle the fish with a little Maldon or *fleur de sel* best quality coarse salt and with a little freshly milled pepper.

> You will find smoking fish at home much easier following this method than you ever imagined. The fish must not touch the wood shavings and should rest on a rack or raised, slotted aluminium disc. Sawdust for smoking can be obtained from a smokery supplier or a reputable small-scale sawmill; fruitwood (e.g. apple wood) can also used. Orange-fleshed sweet potatoes have a sweeter and more flavoursome flesh than the white-fleshed variety.

Raw bream salad, bread crumble, grated lemon zest dressing

To serve 4

For the crumble
1 large, oven-baked (i.e. not steam-baked) white loaf to yield 250 g (9 oz) breadcrumbs
250 g (9 oz) butter, softened at room temperature
250 g (9 oz) plain flour
salt

For the raw bream salad
500 g (1 lb) absolutely fresh fillets of gilt-head bream with its skin, scales removed
olive oil
3 blanched and skinned tomatoes (see recipe on p. 56) finely diced
1 bunch chives
small bunch fresh coriander
juice of 2 lemons
salt, freshly ground pepper

To serve
2 small cartons natural yoghurt
finely grated zest of 1 untreated, unsprayed lemon
best quality coarse salt, freshly ground pepper

Bread crumble

Cut off all the crusts from the bread; cut the interior or 'crumb' into thick slices and spread out on the racks of the oven, preheated to 90 °C (gas mark 3) to bake very gently for approximately 1 hour or until dry and pale golden brown. Place in the food processor and process to fine breadcrumbs. Turn up the oven temperature to 170 °C (gas mark 5–6).

Using the tips of your fingers or a utensil (a pastry blender), combine the butter (softened at room temperature) with the flour until it has the classic crumble consistency. Add 250 g (9 oz) of the breadcrumbs and a little salt; mix briefly together. Place very small mounds of this mixture, pinched into shape to make them hold firm, spaced out on a baking sheet and cook in the oven for 10 minutes or until pale golden brown. Set aside in a warm, dry place.

Raw bream salad

Remove the skin from the bream fillets. Cover a baking sheet with a sheet of greaseproof paper, lightly brush the surface with olive oil and spread the skin out on it. Cover with another sheet of lightly oiled greaseproof paper and then place another baking sheet on top. Cook in a preheated oven at 160 °C (gas mark 6) for about 15–20 minutes, or until the skin is dry and crunchy. Alternatively, cook the bream skin in a non-stick frying pan with a very little olive oil over a gentle heat until crisp, but the skin must still be kept flat: cover with oiled greaseproof paper (oiled side against the fish skin) and place the bottom of a heavy saucepan that fits neatly into the frying pan on top of the paper. Check the skin from time to time; this second method should take no longer than 15 minutes; when it is crisp and

crunchy, leave to cool and then set aside, uncovered, in a warm, dry place.

Dice the bream fillets. Marinate them for 5 minutes in a bowl of salted water. Snip or chop the chives finely and take the coriander leaves off their stalks. Set both aside. Drain the diced fish very thoroughly; mix it with the diced tomato, lemon juice, chives, coriander leaves and 100 ml (3½ fl oz) olive oil. Add extra seasoning to taste.

To serve

Use small, fairly deep dishes or Japanese bowls in which to serve this first course: place a generous tablespoonful of diced fish salad in each dish and sprinkle with a layer of the crumble. On top of the crumble, drizzle a scant teaspoonful of plain yoghurt. Decorate with a pinch of finely grated lemon zest, sprinkle with a little freshly ground pepper and a pinch of coarse salt (*fleur de sel* or Maldon) and then garnish with a piece of the crisped skin.

> You can cut down on preparation time by using good quality (not artificially coloured) commercially prepared breadcrumbs. Use only the very freshest fish; do not use farmed bream; gilthead bream is one of the best but you can also use sea bream, dentex or any true member of the bream family. You can use fresh lime juice and zest instead of lemon.

Western Mediterranean

It is hardly surprising that our cooking bears a recognizably regional imprint, since this is the environment, in its widest sense, in which we have been immersed from childhood. Spain, southern France, Italy and their islands make up the western Mediterranean. Languedoc is thought of as looking towards Spain, while Provence appears more drawn towards Italy, but each of these two regions has its own, unique character, with their respective frontiers being bounded by narrow stretches of land that also possess their own strong personalities. Roussillon is the conduit through which Catalonia's influence reaches France. Even the Comté of Nice, despite its proximity, is more Genoese than Provencal in character: here, the focus is on green vegetables, ravioli, and pesto made with fresh herbs in much the same way as in Genoa and in Savona. At the heart of this region lies the Camargue: peaceful, inscrutable, watching over its wild white horses and herds of cattle.

Above: *displays of pawpaws and oranges in a market in Madeira.*
Left: *a truly Latin combination of colours and atmosphere in the bar at the Compagnie des Comptoirs in Montpellier.*

Montpellier is very close to the Camargue, at the centre of Midi tradition and culture. Thus placed, we realize how much these differing areas have in common.

A certain way of life

Here we find squares shaded by large plane trees and people indulging in endless, desultory conversation over glasses of *anis del Mono*, *pastis* or *anisette*. Nibbling *tapas* in Spain, or *antipasti* in Italy, is the western way of observing the ritual of 'little dishes' so beloved throughout the Mediterranean basin. A siesta is taken during the early afternoon, the better to enjoy oneself – or do business – in the evening. Shops stay open till late. The streets teem with life, especially after nightfall; cool gardens hide behind sturdy walls; and pots of basil flourish on window sills for all to admire. The air of nonchalance is more apparent than real: the sun may sap people's physical energy, but not their wits. On the waterfront, sea urchins, or violets, are consumed with chilled

white wine to the sound of the lapping sea. Fish are grilled in the open air over fires of vine prunings lit between stones. Wine-producing villages are redolent of grape *marc* and the scent of *belles-de-nuit*, those fragrant jalapa flowers that bloom at night. The shared treasures of this world are olive oil, almonds, vines, honey, anchovies, tuna, tomatoes, crystallized fruits, and rich, syrupy wines oxidized to a carefully calculated degree; the patisseries are full of the scent of orange peel in Spain and bitter almonds in Italy. Tomatoes, figs, grapes and pears are savoured with fresh, white cheeses: ricotta, brocciu (from Corsica), brousse niçoise (ewe's milk cheese), mozzarella, mild Provolone. The stronger, harder cheeses such as Parmesan and pecorino accompany pasta dishes; Spanish manchego cheese is enjoyed as a *tapa*, with slices of *membrillo* (pieces of quince jelly).

Our gastronomic points of reference

In our cooking, acknowledgements of our debt to Spain and Italy recur constantly, like affectionate winks of recognition. From Spain we have adopted Iberian raw, cured ham, amazingly tender and sweet – even the fat is a delicacy. We make gaspacho with jellied tomato juice or with pineapple flesh, since it is essential to maintain the freshness and lightness of this first course inspired by the Andalusian sun. We have also adopted a Spanish cooking technique, that of grilling *à la plancha* on a griddle with shallow ridges, the ideal way to sear and seal in all the flavour of meats, fish, crustaceans, vegetables and even fruits. We use this method too to grill asparagus and *parillada* steak, the juicy and flavoursome rib-of-beef cut that is only to be found at its best between the Camargue and Gibraltar. We also cook one of our signature dishes *à la plancha*: squid with lemon confit, an enduring favourite on our menu.

Travelling eastwards, towards Italy, we reinterpret the classic dishes of the coast of Languedoc and Provence. Hot onion tart is our version of Nice's *pissaladière*; garnished with fresh tomato and virtually raw sardines that are given the briefest cooking, a mere heating through in a very hot oven. Our mixed vegetable tart is enhanced by *pistou*, the Italo-Niçoise sauce that we also prepare with rocket leaves, an archetypal Italian salad herb if ever there was one. The little *poivrades* or violet artichokes that have such an intense flavour are served as an antipasto or as a freshly prepared puree accompanied by slices of raw baby artichokes. We also pay tribute to the cheeses that come from the other side of the Alps: ricotta beaten to a frothy lightness with dried vine fruits, grilled Provolone, mozzarella served with roast tomatoes, Parmesan shavings scattered over salads. And, of course, pasta – without which there could be no authentic Mediterranean cuisine – but we reserve the right to translate lasagne into our own dialect by introducing layers of fresh vegetables that have been stir fried in a wok… and beckons us much farther towards the east.

Above: *the sea urchin, a little invertebrate that protects itself with its spines; deep inside are the orange gonads or coral, tasting delicately of iodine and of the sea, that are savoured throughout the Mediterranean area.*

Chilled mousseline of sweet potato, langoustines and seafood aspic with crème fraîche topping

To serve 4

For the langoustines
12 large langoustines
2 tbsps olive oil
1 carrot, diced
1 medium-sized onion, diced
1 leek, diced
1 celery stalk, diced
1 tomato, peeled, de-seeded and chopped
1 bouquet garni
2 egg whites
100 g (3½ oz) extra langoustine flesh (or white fish)
1 small onion, thinly sliced
1 leek, sliced into thin rounds
1 carrot, sliced into thin rounds
6 gelatine leaves
salt, ground white pepper

Mousseline of sweet potato
4 sweet potatoes (orange flesh)
2 tbsps crème fraiche, stiffly beaten
a pinch of caster sugar
salt, ground white pepper

For the artichoke salad
2 young violet artichokes
juice of 1 lemon
3 tbsps olive oil
1 tomato
small bunch of chives, snipped
salt, freshly ground white pepper

To garnish
100 ml (3½ fl oz) crème fraiche, stiffly beaten
a few drops of lemon juice
freshly ground white pepper

Langoustines and seafood aspic

Take the heads off the langoustines before peeling them; keep the heads and shells. Slit down the back of the langoustines with the tip of a small, sharp knife and remove the dark-coloured intestinal tract. Leave to cool.

Fry the langoustines' heads and shells gently in the olive oil in a saucepan; add the cleaned, diced vegetable, the chopped tomato and the bouquet garni. Continue frying gently while stirring for a few minutes, then add sufficient water to cover the contents of the pan completely. Bring slowly to the boil, cover and simmer for approximately 30 minutes. Leave to cool, then strain through a fine sieve.

Return this fish stock to the cleaned saucepan, add the peeled langoustines and poach them for 2 minutes; remove them from the stock, rinse very briefly in cold water and set aside. Clarify the stock: place the egg whites, the 100 g (3½ oz) extra langoustine flesh or white filleted fish and the second batch of prepared, thinly sliced vegetables in a food processor; process until very smoothly blended. Add this mixture to the fish stock, bring to the boil and simmer for 20 minutes over a low heat, stirring gently during the first few minutes.

Gently pour the stock through a fine mesh, conical (chinois) sieve; add seasoning to taste. Measure out 1 litre (1¾ pints) of the hot stock and add the softened gelatine leaves. Leave to stand, away from the heat and when the gelatine has completely dissolved, pour the clarified stock into a stainless steel or glass bowl and chill in the refrigerator.

Cooking the sweet potatoes

Boil the unpeeled sweet potatoes for approximately 30 minutes. Drain thoroughly, peel and sieve. Season with salt and pepper, transfer to a bowl and chill in the refrigerator.

Artichoke salad

Trim the artichokes (see recipe on page 44), placing them in a bowl of cold water acidulated with lemon juice to prevent discolouration. Dice the artichokes finely and sprinkle with lemon juice. Add the olive oil, salt and pepper and mix thoroughly. Add the peeled, de-seeded and diced tomato and the snipped chives.

Mousseline of sweet potato

Stir the 2 tablespoons of stiffly beaten crème fraîche into the pureed sweet potato. Season to taste, adding the sugar if necessary.

To serve

Beat the remaining crème fraiche with a few drops of lemon juice.

Serve in glass coupes or bowls: place 2 tablespoons of sweet potato in each bowl, cover with a layer of diced artichoke salad and place 3 chilled langoustines on top of each serving. Add the langoustine aspic and top with 1 teaspoon of acidulated crème fraiche. Grind a little pepper on top and serve chilled.

This is a starter for a special occasion. Make sure you use very fresh raw langoustines or the best deep frozen ones available. Langoustines are often marketed as Dublin Bay prawns or Norway lobsterettes. For a real treat, add 1 scant teaspoon of Sevruga caviar to each serving, placed on top of the dab of lemon-flavoured crème fraîche.

Langoustines with thyme flowers, baby fennel and radish salad, horseradish vinaigrette

To serve 4

Having removed the crustaceans' heads, use small, pointed scissors to snip down the back of each langoustine, stopping just short of the tail flippers. Remove the shell and extract the black or dark grey intestinal tract; leave the tail flippers attached, intact (see note at end of method). Slice the red onion very finely, place in a bowl and add the coarse salt (use the best: fleur de sel or Maldon). Mix briefly and leave to draw out the moisture from the onions for 1 hour at room temperature, then blot the onions dry with a clean cloth or paper towels and set aside.

Horseradish vinaigrette

Mix the vinegar, salt, pepper, horseradish and olive oil.

Baby fennel and radish salad

Pinch off the flowers from the bunch of fresh thyme.

Peel off the outermost layer from the baby fennel bulbs with a potato peeler and peel or scrub the radishes if wished. Slice very thinly, using a mandoline cutter, very sharp knife or slicer attachment on a food processor. Add the prepared red onions and dress with horseradish vinaigrette to taste; sprinkle with the thyme flowers.

Cooking the langoustines

Lightly oil a griddle or heavy, non-stick grilling pan with olive oil, and when very hot sear the langoustines, turning once; season with salt and pepper.

To serve

Arrange the fennel and radish salad in the centre of each plate. Surround with a thin ribbon of horseradish vinaigrette and place three langoustines on top of each serving of salad.

To peel the langoustines (also known as Dublin Bay prawns and Norway lobsterettes) quickly and easily, first pull off their heads. Slide the lower blade of a pair of small, pointed scissors under the centre of the ventral (underside) section of the langoustine and cut along the shell towards the tail, which should be left attached for this recipe. Snip along the 'back' of the shell also, exposing the intestinal tract for removal. Use your thumbs to push the cut edges gently apart, releasing the flesh. Freshly grated horseradish is easy to find in large supermarkets and good delicatessens, usually displayed with chilled goods or with relishes such as gherkins...

For the langoustines
12 medium-sized langoustines
1 red onion
best quality coarse salt (*fleur de sel*, Maldon)
olive oil
salt, freshly ground white pepper

For the horseradish vinaigrette
1 tbsp sherry vinegar
scant 1 tsp freshly grated horseradish (see note at end of method)
4 tbsps olive oil
salt, freshly ground white pepper

For the baby fennel and radish salad
8 baby fennel bulbs
12 small pink and white, or red, radishes (preferably oblong variety)
2 small, mild red onions
small bunch of fresh flowering thyme

Flavours of the South of France

fish and seafood

Grilled bream fillets with sesame seed coating, slow-baked tomatoes with olives

2 very fresh, large bream (see
note at end of method),
filleted and skinned
400 ml (14 fl oz) balsamic
vinegar
4 tbsps best quality,
unrefined sesame seed oil
100 g (3½ oz) slow-baked
tomato (recipe on page 60)
100 g (3½ oz) best quality,
small French olives, stoned
4 tbsps olive oil
80 g (2½–3 oz) toasted
sesame seeds
salt, freshly ground pepper

To garnish
4 fresh mint leaves
12 fresh coriander leaves

Reduce the vinegar over a gentle heat until it becomes syrupy (see page 60 for method). Mix the reduced vinegar with the sesame seed oil; chill this dressing in the refrigerator. Preheat the oven to 140 °C (gas mark 4–5). Chop the slow-baked tomatoes and the olives coarsely; mix them together in a heatproof bowl. Add 3 tablespoons of olive oil and warm gently over simmering water. Add a little salt and pepper if wished.

Do not allow the surface of the fish to become too dry; season both sides of each bream fillet with salt and pepper. Turn the fillets so that the side exposed by removing the skin is uppermost and sprinkle liberally with sesame seeds, pressing these down firmly so that they adhere. Heat a very little olive oil in a non-stick frying pan and place the fillets in it, coated side down. Lightly brown on this one side only. Transfer to a lightly oiled, shallow baking tray, coated side uppermost, and cook for 6 minutes (if the fillets are very thick, cook for 2–3 minutes longer).

To serve
Put 2 tablespoonfuls of the tomato and olive mixture in the centre of each plate; place the bream fillets on top of this.
Use scissors to cut the mint and coriander leaves into thin strips. Stir them into the vinaigrette and spoon this dressing all over the fillets.

In China and Japan, food grilled with sesame seeds is very popular: the nutty taste of the sesame seeds and oil is delicious. Mediterranean species of bream, each fish weighing 800 g (1¾ lb) before filleting, such as royal, gilthead, dentex) would normally be used for this recipe; very fresh sea bream is a more readily available alternative. Make sure no stray scales are left behind on the fillets after skinning.

Grilled lobster in the shell, liquorice flavoured carrots, sea urchin coral, spice bread dressing

To serve 4

4 frozen Canadian lobsters, each weighing 500–600 g (1–1¼ lb) thawed weight
olive oil

For the sea urchin cream
100 g (3½ oz) stiffly beaten cream
50 g (2 oz) sea urchin coral
pinch of salt, ground pepper

For the court-bouillon
1 finely sliced carrot
1 medium onion, finely sliced
1 leek (green section only), finely sliced
1 celery stalk
1 bay leaf
1 sprig of fresh thyme
coarse sea salt

For the liquorice carrots
20 baby carrots
50 g (2 oz) unsalted butter
30 g (1 oz) caster sugar
1 small, thin stick of unsweetened 'hard' liquorice
2 tbsps juices from roast meat
1 slice of pain d'épices, very finely crumbled
fresh lemon juice
coarse salt, table salt, freshly ground pepper

To serve
2 short sections cut from a thin 'hard' liquorice stick

Sea urchin cream

If you are able to buy sea urchins, you will need several to yield enough 'coral'. Break up the coral with a fork; mix with the cream, adding a very small pinch of salt and a little pepper, and chill in the refrigerator.

Making the court-bouillon and poaching the lobsters

Bring plenty of water to the boil in a large, very deep stock pot or saucepan; add the vegetables and flavourings listed for the court-bouillon. Boil for approximately 20 minutes. Put the lobsters into the gently boiling court-bouillon and simmer for no longer than 3–4 minutes after the liquid returns to a gentle boil. Take them out of the court-bouillon and plunge them immediately into a large bowl of iced water (use ice cubes). Detach the heads from the rest of the lobsters; cut the tails lengthwise in half, along the centre of their backs, slicing right through them using a heavy, sharp knife; loosen the flesh from the shell but do not detach it completely; set aside.

Liquorice flavoured carrots

Peel the carrots, leaving a very short length of their stalks attached; boil them in a large pan of salted water (allow 12 g or scant ½ oz of salt for each litre or 1½ pints of water) until tender but still with a little 'bite' left in them; drain and refresh in iced water. Drain again and glaze them by frying them gently in a saucepan or deep frying pan with half the butter, the sugar and the liquorice stick. When they are lightly browned, transfer them to a heated dish; add the meat juices (or diluted very good

quality meat extract) to the pan and scrape with a wooden spoon over the heat to loosen the cooking deposits. Stir in the pain d'épices (spiced honey bread) crumbs. Add the remaining butter (as a solid piece) and beat with a balloon whisk as it melts; season with salt and pepper and add a few drops of lemon juice. Set aside.

Grilled lobsters

Drizzle a little olive oil over the surfaces of the lobster flesh in the half shells; place them under a hot grill until the flesh has firmed up and stiffened; do not cook for more than a few minutes or they will be dry and tough.

To serve

Arrange 5 carrots on each plate, coat with the reserved cooking juices; place a half lobster on their tapering ends, tip the flesh to one side in the shell, towards the thicker end of the carrots, allowing room to place a rounded spoonful of the sea urchin cream in the shell (see facing page); place a small piece of liquorice on top of this scoop of cream and surround the lobster and carrots with a thin trickle of olive oil.

This dish is a pleasure to look at, with the white, red-mottled lobster flesh resting on its scarlet shell. Serve these lightly cooked lobsters immediately they are ready.

Scallop brochettes with Serrano raw cured ham, grilled lettuce hearts, roasted tomatoes and balsamic dressing

Cut each Serrano ham slice into 4 pieces. Assemble the brochettes, starting with a scallop and alternate with pieces of the ham: allow 3 scallops for each brochette and 2 pieces of ham. Rinse the lettuce hearts, drain well and blot dry with a clean cloth or kitchen towels; cut them into quarters.

Vinaigrette

Heat the roasting juices (very good quality meat or chicken essence, diluted, could be used if necessary); stir in the reduced balsamic vinegar and the hazelnut oil with a wooden spoon; season to taste.

Cooking the lettuces and brochettes

Heat a very little olive oil in the griddle or grilling pan and cook the lettuces over a fairly high heat, turning them several times; season them with salt and pepper and transfer to a heated dish. Heat a very little fresh olive oil on the griddle or in the pan and when very hot cook the brochettes, allowing only a few seconds on each side to allow them to brown lightly and barely cook through.

To serve

Pan-roast the tomatoes for a few minutes in a little olive oil, in a covered pan.
Using oval plates if you have them, arrange 2 quarters of lettuce heart on each, with a tomato, sprinkle with the warm balsamic vinegar dressing. Place a brochette on top of the lettuce hearts and garnish, if wished, with a couple of Parmesan cheese shavings.

If anything, Little Gem lettuces taste better cooked than raw and they are widely available, imported from Spain. Use the delicious bright orange coral from the scallops to add flavour and colour to a seafood dish or a white fish recipe; it will keep for 24 hours if refrigerated.

Squid and Mediterranean vegetables seared à la plancha, lemon confit

For the seared squid
600 g (1¼ lb) fresh, small squid
30 ml (1 fl oz) olive oil
salt, freshly ground pepper

For the lemon confit
2 untreated lemons
250 ml (9 fl oz) water
150 g (5 oz) granulated or caster sugar

For the Mediterranean vegetables 'a la plancha'
2 baby violet artichokes
juice of 1 lemon
1 red sweet pepper
1 small courgette
4 large, bulbous spring onions
olive oil
salt, freshly ground pepper

For the lemon confit dressing
juice of 1 lemon
100 ml (3½ fl oz) olive oil
1 ripe, deep-red tomato
small bunch of chives
salt, freshly ground pepper

Clean and prepare the squid, rinsing them very thoroughly under cold running water; drain them on a clean cloth; chill them in the refrigerator until needed.

Lemon confit

Boil the water and sugar together to make a light sugar syrup. Rinse the lemons under the cold tap and slice them very thinly without peeling them. Add these slices to the sugar syrup. Cook over a gentle heat until the lemon slices are translucent. Drain and set aside.

Mediterranean vegetables 'a la plancha'

Clean, trim and rinse all the vegetables. Prepare the artichokes using a very sharp, small knife to 'turn' them (see method in recipe on page 38, first paragraph). As you prepare each artichoke, immediately rub it with lemon juice to prevent discolouration and then add to a bowl of cold water acidulated with lemon juice.

Peel the sweet pepper with a potato peeler, removing only the thin outer skin; remove and discard the seeds, stalk and pale parts inside before cutting the flesh into large, square pieces.

Cut the courgettes into rounds; trim the spring onions (use small, imported fresh white onions still attached to their green stalks if available).

Lemon confit dressing

Chop the lemon slices with a heavy knife, place them in a salad bowl and add the lemon juice, the olive oil and a little of the sugar syrup in which the lemons were cooked, and season with salt and pepper.

Blanch the tomato for a few seconds in boiling water, then drain and peel it; remove the seeds and cut the flesh into small dice. Chop or snip the chives finely. Add the chives and tomato to the lemon confit dressing.

Cooking vegetables and squid Spanish style 'a la plancha' (searing)

Heat a griddle or a heavy frying pan over a high heat, pour in a little olive oil and brown the vegetables, cooking each type separately. Sprinkle them with salt and pepper and keep them hot.

Dry the surface of the griddle or frying pan with kitchen towels; pour in a very little fresh olive oil and return to a high heat. Sear the squid so that they brown lightly but are only just cooked. You can use the tentacles as well as the bodies if you buy baby squid. Season with salt and pepper.

To assemble the dish

Arrange the vegetables on each plate, alternating the colours; place the squid on top and surround with lemon confit dressing.

> If overcooked, grilled squid will become very tough and chewy. Searing them for a very short time over a high heat until they are only just cooked through leaves them tender and brings out their flavour.

Fried white fish fillets, leeks and almonds vinaigrette, fresh white cheese shake

For the fried fish fillets
4 very fresh hake or whiting
fillets, each weighing 140 g
(approximately 5 oz)
3 tbsps plain flour
2 tbsps olive oil
juice of ½ lemon
salt, freshly ground pepper

**For the fresh cream
cheese shake**
240 g (½ lb) very soft, moist
fromage blanc or
fromage frais
100 ml (3½ fl oz) milk
juice of ½ lemon
1 tbsp olive oil
salt, freshly ground white
pepper

For the leeks vinaigrette
24 thin, baby leeks
small bunch fresh mint
4 'petals' of slow baked
tomato (see recipe on
page 54)
3 tbsps olive oil
juice of 1 lemon
1 tbsp peeled almonds,
coarsely chopped
coarse salt, table salt
freshly ground pepper

Fresh cheese shake

Process all the ingredients in a blender and chill in the refrigerator. La Faiselle fromage frais or other very soft white, fresh cheeses such as demi-sel or Petit Suisse are all suitable.

Leeks vinaigrette

Trim the leeks, removing the outermost layer; wash thoroughly; tie them together in a bundle with two well-spaced pieces of string and boil for 2 minutes in a large saucepan of boiling water; allow 30 g (1 oz) salt for each litre (1¾ pints) water. Remove from the pan and lower into a large bowl of iced water (use ice cubes).
Blanch the mint leaves for a few seconds only in the salted boiling water; rinse under the cold tap and blot dry with kitchen paper towels. Cut them into fairly broad strips. Dice the slow-baked tomatoes finely.
Mix the olive oil and the lemon juice.

Fish fillets

Pick out any remaining bones from the fish with tweezers. Coat the fillets lightly with flour, shaking off excess. Fry briefly in hot olive oil in a frying pan, turning once; when they are cooked, sprinkle with the lemon juice and a little salt. Keep hot.

To serve

Drain the leeks and remove the string; reheat them gently over a low heat in a non-stick pan. Sprinkle with the vinaigrette, the mint leaves, diced tomato and the almonds. Transfer 6 leeks to each plate, spoon the remaining vinaigrette and other ingredients from the pan over them. Place the fillet of fish to one side of the leeks and serve with a glass of the fresh cheese shake.

> Careful timing is the essence of success for this simple recipe: the leeks should be tender but still crisp and the fish fillets should be just cooked through, still moist and firm. Use fromage blanc (very fresh white cheese) that is 'sloppy', almost the consistency of yoghurt, for this recipe.

Crunchy pineapple and prawn fried sandwich with herb stuffing

To serve 4

For the crunchy pineapple and prawn fried sandwich
12 large, pink Mediterranean prawns
1 large pineapple
olive oil
salt, freshly ground pepper

For the herb stuffing
1 oven-baked white loaf (i.e. not steam-baked)
approximately 300 ml (10–11 fl oz) milk
bunch of fresh coriander
200 ml (7 fl oz) olive oil
pinch of Espelette chilli powder
juice of ½ lemon
salt, freshly ground pepper

For the caramelized balsamic vinegar
700 ml (1¼ pints) balsamic vinegar

For the egg and breadcrumb coating
2 tbsps plain flour
2 eggs
2–3 heaped tbsps freshly made breadcrumbs (see method)
salt, freshly ground pepper

Cut all the crust away from a slightly stale white loaf; spread the crusts out on a baking sheet and dry in the oven (at 100 °C – gas mark 3–4) until dry and crunchy. Reduce to fine breadcrumbs in a food processor. Meanwhile break up the soft inside of the loaf into fairly small pieces and place in a bowl. Add sufficient milk to cover and leave to soak. Peel the pineapple and cut 8 thin, rectangular slices measuring 8 x 4 cm (3 x 1½ in). Place these on kitchen paper on a large plate and sprinkle lightly with salt to draw out their excess moisture. Set aside.

Caramelized balsamic vinegar
Reduce the balsamic vinegar in a heavy-bottomed saucepan over a gentle heat until it becomes syrupy and coats the bottom of the pan lightly when the latter is tipped to one side.

Herb bread stuffing
Place the coriander leaves, the olive oil and a pinch of salt in the food processor and blend. Squeeze out excess moisture from the milk-soaked bread and add to the mixture, with the Espelette chilli pepper powder; process until very well blended and uniformly pale green. Add a little lemon juice, and more seasoning if needed. If the mixture is very stodgy, add a very little milk and process briefly.

Crunchy pineapple, prawn sandwich
Blot dry the rectangles of pineapple with fresh kitchen paper; use a knife to spread a thin layer of the herb stuffing over the pineapple slices. Cook the prawns briefly in a little hot olive oil over a high heat, season with a little salt and pepper and blot dry on kitchen paper. Cut the prawns lengthwise in two, or three,

depending on their size. Spread them out evenly on half the pineapple slices. Cover with remaining slices and press lightly so the prawns are securely sandwiched between two layers of herb stuffing.

Coating and frying the sandwiches
Spread the flour out on a large plate; beat the eggs lightly and pour into another, deeper, plate; spread the home-made breadcrumbs out on a third plate. Carefully coat each sandwich all over with flour, then dip in the beaten egg; finally coat with breadcrumbs. Have 2 tablespoons of very hot olive oil ready in a large, non-stick frying pan; fry the sandwiches on both sides until they are well browned.

To serve
Surround each sandwich with a trickle of the caramelized balsamic vinegar.

Make sure the crusts are totally dried out before you make the breadcrumbs in the food processor; if you have made more than you need for the 'sandwiches', store in an airtight jar: home-made breadcrumbs are much better than shop-bought ones.
If you use North Sea prawns which are smaller, double the quantity. Buy unpeeled prawns and peel them yourself: they have more flavour.

Southern Mediterranean

Lapping the shores of the Maghreb, the Mediterranean makes its geographical landfall in North Africa while coming into contact with the East by an accident of history. The western part of North Africa has frequently been invaded and here disparate peoples, languages, ways of life and religions have lived side by side – and sometimes clashed: Berbers, Kabyles, Phoenicians, Greeks, Romans, Arabs, Turks, Jews, Christians, Muslims and, later, the French colonists. This cultural brew has rendered the Maghreb one of the most complex regions in the world. It is only natural that its gastronomy should reflect this complexity, mirroring the cultural layers piled on top of one another, like the many layers of pastry in a *pastilla*. It also reflects the country's varying climate: hot near the coast, more bracing in the foothills of the Atlas mountains and on the plateaux, harsh in the heart of the high mountains. Then there is the desert, covering a vast area of Morocco, Algeria and

Above: *the souk or great central market in Marrakech.*
Facing page, left: *these Far-Eastern paper lanterns add to the oriental ambiance at the Compagnie des Comptoirs.*

Above: *sweetened tea with fresh mint is much more than a culinary tradition in Morocco. It is part of the ritual of social intercourse, a courtesy always extended to guest and friend alike, and to accept and appreciate its taste and scent is an indispensable part of any relationship.*

southern Tunisia. This region's culinary traditions also reflect the richness and diversity of its flora and fauna: the coastal seas are full of fish – Agadir is the world's most important sardine-fishing port – while goats and sheep graze the upland pastures, and down in the plains olive and orange groves, vineyards and orchards stretch out over the landscape.

Liquid gold and aromatics

Of all Maghreb cuisines, we find Moroccan cooking the most fascinating. Morocco is a world apart, safeguarding the treasures of its ancient history through a culture that is highly evolved, secretive and sometimes disconcerting: hidden among the high valleys of the Atlas or in the innermost palace courtyards, it demands perseverance to discover. Once the threshold has been crossed, however, what cultural riches are revealed! Moroccan hospitality is informed by age-old custom, starting with a welcome of bread and *amlou* (almond paste sweetened with honey and flavoured with argan oil). Argan oil is a product unique to Morocco, typical of the Sous plain, Agadir, Essaouira and Taroudannt, being extracted from the nuts of the wild argan tree which grows only in the south of Morocco. Rare and much sought after, it has an enchanting, musky aroma. Production of the oil is still a cottage industry, in which only women are involved. The other liquid gold treasure of Morocco is olive oil; Moroccan cooking does indeed seem to be typified by various shades of gold. Those precious golden oils, oranges and lemons, spices such as turmeric that imparts its colour to the aromatic spice mixture *ras-el-hanout*, and, above all, saffron – all find their place in the royal tradition of cooking. These glimmers of gold give Moroccan cuisine its vivid, colourful appearance, enhancing the freshness of the vegetables which are the particular pride of Fez, offsetting the purity and blandness of couscous and highlighting the delicious aromas of meats that have been slow-cooked in tajines with honey, spices, preserved lemons, dates and dried fruits. The *pastilla*, a pie made with flaky pastry, filled with a sweet-savoury mixture of onions, pigeon, hard-boiled eggs and almonds, symbolizes all the splendour of this palace gastronomy, prepared by highly skilled cooks.

The delights of paradise lost

Such a rich culinary tradition, so full of scents and aromas, that delicately combines the savoury and the sweet, has been nourished, in common with other great cuisines, by foreign influences and by the contributions of immigrants far back in time. Drawing on two thousand years of history, Morocco's gastronomy was born when the native Berber cuisine came into contact with the aristocratic tradition of medieval Andalusia, that Spanish paradise lost, mourned in the hearts of Muslims, a golden age that preceded the *Reconquista*, when the south of the Iberian peninsula was reconquered during the

fifteenth century by the Catholic monarchs Ferdinand and Isabella. After the reconquest, many Muslims who were forced to leave Spain took refuge in Morocco while, at the same time, the Sephardic Jews who had also been expelled from Spain brought with them their knowledge of the art of eating well. This era, known as 'Al Andalus', persists to this day in the folk memory of the Maghrebians as a golden age when tolerance and civilization were a way of life, when science – particularly the branch of medicine – flourished and the cuisine of the region was one of the most exquisite ever known. But of course this perfection was not a product of spontaneous generation. The Andalusians had themselves borrowed a great deal from the East, especially from Persia and from Byzantium – notably the essentials of their dietary and culinary principles: the sweet-savoury mixtures; combining meat and poultry with fresh fruits and with dried fruits; simmering over very low heat; the use of honey, of cinnamon, saffron and scented waters such as rose water and orange-flower water, all of which originated from Persia. This is yet another example of how such cuisines, apparently steeped in immutable tradition, have developed as a result of travel and cultural cross-fertilization.

Above: *a grocer and spice merchant's stall, around 1919, in a souk, or market in Fez. A traditional, unchanging choice of aromatic and appetizing foodstuffs: spices, dates, garlands of figs, and all sorts of flours and cereals.*

Roast knuckles of lamb and salsify puree with hazelnut milk, rich gravy and crushed hazelnuts

For the knuckles of lamb
4 knuckles of lamb
2 tbsps grape seed oil
2 carrots, finely sliced
1 medium onion, finely sliced
1 leek, white part only, finely sliced
thyme, bay leaf
1 litre (¾ pints) chicken stock
1 tbsp sherry vinegar
20 g (scant 1 oz) butter

For the salsify puree
350 g (¾ lb) salsify
juice of 1 lemon
1 white, floury potato approximately 100g (3½ oz)
20 g (scant 1 oz) butter
pinch of sugar
salt, freshly ground white pepper

To garnish
50 g (2 oz) whole hazelnuts

For the hazelnut milk
100 ml (3½ fl oz) full-cream milk
1 tbsp single cream
1 tbsp hazelnut oil
salt, freshly ground pepper

For the salad
100 g (3½ oz) baby spinach leaves
1 tbsp sherry vinegar
2 tbsps walnut oil
salt, freshly ground pepper

Braised knuckles of lamb

Preheat the oven to 90 ºC (gas mark 3). Brown the lamb knuckles all over in the olive oil in a large, fairly deep, fireproof casserole dish; add all the flavouring ingredients listed up to, and including, the thyme and bay leaf. Stir and turn and fry gently for 2 minutes before adding the chicken stock and bring to the boil. Transfer to the preheated oven and cook for 2½ hours. Drain all the liquid and juices from the cooked lamb into a bowl for later use. Place the lamb knuckles under a hot grill to caramelize their surfaces.

Salsify puree

Prepare a large bowl of cold water acidulated with plenty of lemon juice, and as you peel each salsify root cut it into short lengths and place immediately in this bowl to prevent discolouration. Cook the salsify with the peeled and chopped potato in a little water with the butter and sugar in a heavy bottomed saucepan. When the salsify and the potatoes are very tender (this will take about 30 minutes), drain and process to a very smooth puree in the food processor. Season to taste.

Garnish

Roast the hazelnuts for about 10 minutes on a baking sheet in the oven, preheated to 180 ºC (gas mark 6). Rub off their fine, papery skins in a clean cloth. Crush them coarsely.

Hazelnut milk

Mix the milk, cream and hazelnut oil in a saucepan. Place over a low heat and season with salt and pepper. Before serving, blend the mixture with a hand-held electric beater.

Rich gravy

Transfer one-quarter of the cooking juices reserved from baking the lamb knuckles to a saucepan and reduce over a moderate heat, uncovered, until thickened to a syrupy, glossy consistency. Add the sherry vinegar, followed by the extra piece of butter. Use a hand-held electric beater to blend the butter into the gravy as it melts. Add salt and pepper to taste.

The salad

Wash and dry the baby spinach leaves, discarding any wilted or damaged leaves; toss them in the vinaigrette of sherry vinegar, walnut oil, salt and pepper.

To serve

Use 2 tablespoons to shape an oval 'quenelle' or dumpling of the salsify puree and place on one side of each plate. Position the spinach salad on the other side and place the lamb knuckle between them. Add a little hazelnut milk and, near the knuckle, some of the gravy. Sprinkle with the crushed toasted hazelnuts.

If you want to make the lamb knuckles look particularly mouth watering, make a caramel with 100 g (3½ oz) caster sugar and when this has melted and started to colour, add a little soy sauce. Brush the cooked, drained knuckle all over with this mixture and then place under the very hot grill, turning regularly, to glaze.

Steak parillada 'smashed' potatoes; shallot, red wine and anchovy sauce

Flavours of the South of France

To serve 4

For the steak *parillada*
4 thick, well-hung, mature prime beef entrecôte steaks
large bunch of fresh white onions (see note)
2 limes
olive oil
salt, freshly ground black pepper
8 wooden skewers for brochettes

For the wine, shallot and anchovy sauce
4 shallots
30 g (1 oz) butter + 20 g (scant 1 oz) to finish sauce
250 ml (9 fl oz) good quality dry red wine
250 ml (9 fl oz) beef stock, preferably home-made, reduced
4 anchovy fillets (preserved in oil)
salt, freshly ground pepper

For the 'smashed' potatoes
600 g (1¼–1½ lb) yellow, waxy or salad potatoes
3 tbsps olive oil
salt, freshly ground black pepper

To serve
2 tbsps olive oil
best quality coarse salt (*fleur de sel*, Maldon)

Wash the potatoes and boil them, unpeeled, until tender in plenty of boiling salted water.

Wine, shallot and anchovy sauce

Peel and chop the shallots very finely. Cook them very gently in 30 g (1 oz) butter until soft but not at all browned. Add the red wine and simmer, uncovered, until all the moisture has evaporated. Add the beef stock and reduce to half its original volume over a low heat. Finish the sauce by adding the anchovies, crushed with a fork, and when they have dissolved add the remaining small, piece of butter, beating with a balloon whisk as it melts into the sauce.

Grilled steak

Peel off the outer layer of the fresh white onions (see note at end of method), trim off the roots and about two-thirds of the stem but leave the onions whole. Reserve 4 of them to garnish the finished dish. Cut the limes lengthwise into quarters. Cut the entrecôte steaks into large pieces (slightly bigger than normal bite size) and thread them on to the skewers, starting with a lime quarter, followed by a piece of steak, then a whole white onion and so on. Prepare 2 brochettes per person.

Smashed potatoes

Peel and place potatoes in a large bowl; use a potato masher or large fork to break them up roughly but do not mash them. Season with salt and pepper; stir in the olive oil. Keep hot.

Grilling the steak

Cook the remaining onions in olive oil in a heavy bottomed saucepan, until they are very tender and golden brown. Season with a little salt and pepper and set aside.

Heat a little olive oil in a very wide heavy, non-stick frying pan or use a griddle; when hot add the brochettes and cook, turning once or twice; cooking time will depend on how rare or well-done you prefer your steak.

To serve

Spoon some of the potatoes on to each plate, garnish with the braised, whole onions. Add the steak brochettes. Pour a thin trickle of wine, shallot and anchovy sauce around the contents of the plate, add a trickle of olive oil and sprinkle a pinch of very good coarse salt over each brochette.

This is a robust dish inspired by the *parilladas* so beloved by the Argentinos, for which full-flavoured meat from young, enire bulls is used, and it is also a reminder of the bullring at Nîmes, and of the Camargue. This recipe is also delicious if the more tender, well-hung entrecôte beefsteak comes, as it ususally does in this country, from a castrated animal Fresh white onions, with large bulbs and their stalks still attached, are being increasingly imported and widely sold. Large, bulbous spring onions (often sold as 'Continental salad onions') may be substituted, as may home-grown fresh shallots, to imitate the authentic young onions grown around Lézignan.

Chicken and chilli pepper tortilla wrap with plain yoghurt and coriander

For the sautéed chicken

4 chicken breasts, skinned

pinch of Espelette chilli

pepper powder

olive oil

salt, freshly ground pepper

For the vegetables

4 large spring onions or fresh

white onions

1 sweet red pepper, skinned

125 g (4 oz) button

mushrooms

1 courgette

1 fresh white onion, with

stalk, or large spring onion or

fresh shallot

small bunch of fresh

coriander

olive oil

salt, freshly ground pepper

To assemble the dish

4 plain corn tortillas (soft)

2 slices raw cured ham

(lean, coarser quality

prosciutto type)

4 tbsps plain yoghurt

4 slow-cooked tomato 'petals'

(see recipe on p. 54)

1 lime, cut lengthwise into

quarters

best coarse salt (*fleur

de sel*, Maldon),

freshly ground pepper

olive oil

Preheat the oven to 160 °C (gas mark 5–6) Cut each tortilla into 3 equal parts; shape each in turn by pressing it over a fairly large pastry cutter or similar utensil, moulding the tortilla into a 'cup' shape (see facing page). Place these in the oven to dry for approximately 10 minutes to 'set' their shape, then keep ready for use in a warm, dry place.

Place the ham slices in a wide, non-stick frying pan, place some non-stick paper on top of them and then weight down with another frying pan or saucepan of the same or slightly smaller diameter. Dry very gently over a very low heat for about 15 minutes; the object is to make the ham very crisp and crunchy – you will need to check it from time to time. Place the crisp (but not at all burnt) ham in the food processor and reduce to a powdery consistency.

Slice the chicken breasts into thick strips. Place them in a bowl and sprinkle them all over with the Espelette chilli powder; add seasoning and leave to flavour for 30 minutes.

The vegetables

Wash, trim and peel all the vegetables. Cut the sweet red pepper into fairly wide julienne strips (having discarded the seeds and inner pith etc.); cut the mushrooms into quarters and dice the courgette. Slice or chop the onion very finely. Take the coriander leaves off their stalks.

Cooking the chicken and vegetables

Heat 2 non-stick frying pans. Pour a very little olive oil into each of them. Gently fry the chicken strips in 1 pan, allowing them to brown lightly; cook the vegetables, one type at a time, in the other pan, starting with the

courgette. Fry the mushrooms and allow them to brown lightly; do likewise with the fresh white onion and spring onions (or your chosen substitute) and with the sweet red pepper. Season to taste. Mix all these ingredients with the chicken and add the coriander leaves.

To serve

Place 3 pieces of tortilla on each plate, concave side uppermost; spoon the chicken and vegetable mixture neatly into each tortilla section. Add 1 tablespoon of plain yoghurt to each serving, sprinkle with some of the powdered raw, cured ham, and decorate with a tomato petal and a lime quarter. Sprinkle with some best quality coarse salt, some freshly ground pepper and surround with a trickle of olive oil.

> The technique of drying out the ham slices is almost the same as for the bream skin (see method on page 70): the slices have to be laid out absolutely flat against the bottom of the non-stick frying pan; cover if wished with greaseproof paper and place another pan on top to keep the slice flat against the surface of the hot pan. When ready, the ham should be dry and crunchy, rather like a crisp, but not discoloured. The tortillas are dried to shape to serve the same purpose as tacos and have an agreeably crisp texture.

Eastern Mediterranean

When a native of southern Europe speaks of the eastern Mediterranean, the reference is not simply to a distant region but also to a mother country. Down the centuries, the Levant and the Occident have reached out towards each other. During the sixth century BC many trading posts were founded by Greek settlers along the coastline of what was to become southern Gaul, at Agde, Marseilles, Hyères, Antibes, Nice; and inland, at Arles and Glanum, and, later, at Aleria in Corsica. Greeks and Phoenicians were for centuries engaged in maritime commerce. The Greek presence in the eastern Mediterranean was relatively short lived, but left traces that are still discernible today, especially in the cooking of the area. Saffron, transported throughout the ancient world by the Phoenicians and highly prized by the Greeks, had already become the world's rarest and most expensive spice. It is still an essential ingredient in traditional recipes such as *tielle*, a speciality of

Above: *Istanbul is usually thought of as the gateway between East and West: an orange sun glows above a boat cruising along the Bosphorus, silhouetted against the coastline of the Turkish capital.*
Facing page:
dried small chillies, ready to add fierce, peppery heat to eastern Mediterranean dishes.

Left: *succulent fresh
vegetables, bursting with
sunshine, displayed in
an eastern
Mediterranean market.*
Right: *in a pool at the
Compagnie des
Comptoirs' premises, a
water lily conjures up
thoughts of secret
gardens in harems, the
fountains of Ottoman
palaces and the
graceful Egyptian lotus.*

Sète (a pie made with saffron-flavoured and coloured cuttlefish), bouillabaisse and rouille. Aioli, which has long been part of the Italian, Spanish and Provençal repertoires, originated in Greece, where it is called *skordhalia* and is served with poached fish and vegetables. Other versions of this cold, garlic-flavoured sauce are found in Turkish, Syrian and Egyptian cooking, one example being *tarator*, which may also contain sesame paste, pounded almonds or walnuts, breadcrumbs and yoghurt, or can simply be made with crushed garlic blended with a little oil, as in the Syrian version.

Origins of bouillabaisse and the Levantine sweet tooth

The bouillabaisse of Marseilles has a Greek ancestor that survives to this day in the form of *kakavia*, a more primitive recipe than its descendant: a selection of fish, including bream, John Dory, moray eel, conger eel and grouper, is simply boiled gently over a low heat with vegetables and potatoes. The soup and the fish are served together as one dish.

For many years the flavours of the eastern Mediterranean have tended to travel westwards. The sophisticated cuisine of Muslim Andalusia was widely renowned in the Middle Ages, being a synthesis of Persian, Arabic and Byzantine influences. Through its recipes the methods and dietary customs of earliest antiquity were passed on to later generations. Subsequently it was the turn of the Ottoman Empire, as the Turks' conquests multiplied and their trading ports proliferated in the Balkans and North Africa, to spread the culinary expertise of the sultans' cooks, as well as the customs and practices contributed by Byzantine cooking which had, in turn, benefited from the legacy of ancient Greece. Those soft and yielding pieces of Turkish delight (*loukoum*) with their aroma of rose petals, pistachio or mastic; the wafer-thin sheets of filo wheat pastry used to make crisp, crunchy sweetmeats; and *kadaif* (very fine vermicelli-like strands of pastry) are found in Turkey, Greece, Syria and the Lebanon, in Egypt and throughout the Maghreb. The confection of Middle-Eastern pastries involves

A spice merchant carefully weighs out some of his precious stock in the Khan and Khaliby souk in Cairo.

alternating sheets of filo pastry or layers of *kadaif* (which have been liberally coated with melted butter) with layers of crushed almonds, pistachios, hazelnuts or other ingredients. Once these pastries have been baked in the oven, they are sprinkled all over with sugar syrup scented with rose petals or orange blossom. They are the inspiration for our own oriental pastries made with pears and almonds. The pleasure of tasty morsels or nibbles is a quintessentially Mediterranean experience. In Spain and Italy, wines and aperitifs are accompanied by *tapas* or *antipasti*, while in the eastern Mediterranean region great importance is attached to similar traditional delicacies. In Turkey these 'little dishes' are known as *meze*, in Syria and Lebanon as *mezze*, in Greece *mezedhes* and in North Africa *kemia*. As with *tapas*, there are countless *meze* recipes, ranging from the simple and unadorned olive or slice of turnip pickled in brine to complex and highly spiced preparations using vegetables, meat and seafood.

Olive oil: from amphorae to earthenware jars and bottles

The eastern Mediterranean is where Orient and Occident meet. No one seems to know exactly where the boundary lies. Perhaps in Greece, the culture of which has a great many oriental characteristics, discernible in its music, poetry and food. Or maybe in Turkey, resolutely Asian but preoccupied by Europe after centuries of intertwined history. One certainty, however, remains: olive oil is the golden thread that runs through all Mediterranean civilizations, with the olive branch being synonymous with peace. Archaeological digs in the area are still unearthing the two-handled, large earthenware jars used for centuries to store olive oil. These lands are home to almond, fig, orange and lemon trees (providing the raw materials for preserved or candied fruits); grape vines, wild herbs, aromatic resins, incense, honey and beeswax. It is customary for the inhabitants to sit in the shade outside their local café and put the world to rights over an aniseed-flavoured drink. This is a world where time moves slowly, like a lazy trickle of olive oil down the side of an earthenware jar.

Grilled fillet steaks, Montpellier butter, onion compote, beetroot crisps

To serve 4

4 tournedos (filet mignon
beef fillet steaks) about
160 g (5–6 oz) each
4 thin slices of dry-cured
smoked streaky bacon
best quality coarse salt

For the onion compote
6 mild white onions
20 g (scant 1 oz) butter
100 g (3½ oz) caster sugar
50 ml (2 fl oz) balsamic
vinegar
table salt, best quality coarse
salt, freshly ground pepper

For the Montpellier sauce
bunch of watercress
bunch flat-leaved parsley
small bunch chervil
small bunch chives
50 g (2 oz) baby spinach
leaves, blanched and drained
4 shallots, peeled and very
finely chopped
4 small gherkins
2 anchovy fillets
20 g (scant 1 oz) capers
3 small garlic cloves
1 egg yolk
pinch of Cayenne pepper
(optional)
200 g (7 oz) butter, softened
salt, ground white pepper

For the beetroot crisps
1 raw beetroot, peeled
600 g (1¼ lb) caster sugar
1 litre (1¾ pints) water

Onion compote

Slice the onions very finely and cook gently in the butter over a low heat. When they become translucent (do not allow to brown), add the sugar and the balsamic vinegar. Continue cooking slowly until the vinegar has evaporated. Continue cooking over the lowest possible heat, stirring now and then, for about 1 hour. The onions should have reduced to a very soft, mushy consistency; remove from the heat, season to taste.

Montpellier butter

Take all the fresh herb leaves off their stems; place all the ingredients except for the butter in a food processor and process to a paste. Add the butter and process until the mixture is light and 'fluffy'. Set aside in a cool place.

Beetroot crisps

Preheat the oven to 120 ºC (gas mark 3). Cut the beetroot into very thin slices. Heat the water and sugar and boil briefly to make a light syrup. Add the wafer-thin beetroot slices to the syrup, allow them to soak in it for a few minutes, then remove them and spread out in a single layer on non-stick greaseproof or silicone paper on a baking sheet. Put them in the oven to dry out and crisp for approximately 1 hour.

Cooking and serving

Dry-fry the streaky bacon in a non-stick frying pan until it is very crisp. Keep hot.
Grill the steaks, or fry them in a very little oil: the cooking time will depend on how rare you like your steak. Sprinkle with a little coarse salt when cooked. Heat the Montpellier butter with a very little water in a small saucepan and then blend with a hand-held electric mixer. Spoon some of the onion compote onto each plate, place a steak on top and pour some of the Montpellier butter sauce around and on top of each steak. Garnish with beetroot crisps and with the crisp bacon.

Montpellier butter is a very old sauce recipe that is usually served with grilled fish and various types of cold meat. Some recipes include the anchovies, some not, but plenty of fresh herbs are always essential. In our part of France, we always make the onion compote with local onions, from Lézignan: large, fresh, white onions that have a particularly sweet taste when cooked slowly for a long time. Use the mildest onions you can buy and, if necessary, cheat by adding a pinch of caster sugar.

La Compagnie's warm, cool and Arctic-zone cappuccino; brownies

For the thick hot chocolate
180 g (6½ oz) best unsweetened plain or bitter chocolate
100 g (3½ oz) milk chocolate
280 ml (10 fl oz) milk
160 ml (5½ fl oz) single cream

For the vanilla-flavoured Chantilly cream
500 ml (18 fl oz) whipping cream
70 g (2½–3 oz) icing sugar
½ vanilla pod

For the coffee granita
480 ml (17 fl oz) hot espresso coffee
80 ml (2½ fl oz) hot, diluted chicory essence
60 g (2 oz) caster sugar

For the brownies
80 g (3 oz) unsalted butter +
2 tsps extra for the baking tin
120 g (4 oz) plain flour + 1 tsp extra for the baking tin
300 g (11 oz) caster sugar
4 eggs
40 g (1½ oz) pure, unsweetened cocoa powder
100 g (3½ oz) pecan nuts, coarsely chopped
100 g (3½ oz) good quality chocolate drops or chips

Decorate with
4 fresh mint leaves
1 tbsp coarsely crushed cocoa beans

Thick chocolate (warm ganache)
Chop the two types of chocolate and mix them together in a heatproof bowl. Bring the milk and cream to the boil, pour this onto the chopped chocolate. Stir carefully with a wooden spoon until completely smooth and glossy. Keep warm over hot (not boiling) water.

Vanilla-flavoured Chantilly cream
Mix the cream and the icing sugar, stir in the seeds from the half vanilla pod (slit the pod and scrape out the seeds with the tip of a knife). Pour through a very fine mesh sieve. Chill in a bowl. When very cold, beat until stiff with a hand-held electric beater; return to the refrigerator.

Coffee granita
Mix all the ingredients while the coffee is still hot. Leave to cool completely; place in the freezer. Just before serving the 'cappuccino', break up the frozen mixture by running the prongs of a fork along the surface, resulting in coffee ice crystals.

Making and baking the brownies
Preheat the oven to 180 °C (gas mark 6). Use the extra butter to grease a fairly deep rectangular cake tin; dust the greased tin with the extra flour, tipping out excess. Beat the butter vigorously with the caster sugar until very pale and light, beat in the eggs one by one and then stir in the sifted flour and cocoa. Fold in the pecan nuts and the chocolate drops. Turn this cake mixture into the prepared cake tin and bake for 30–35 minutes or until a skewer inserted into it just comes out clean. The brownie cake should be fairly firm when done but still moist and almost 'fluffy'; remove from the oven and cut into squares in the tin while hot. Leave to cool a little and take them out of the tin while they are still slightly warm. They will turn 'fudgy' as they cool.

Assembling the warm, cool and Arctic-zone cappuccino
Fill each of 4 glasses one-third full with the thick, warm chocolate; fill the next third with a layer of Chantilly cream; spoon the coffee granita on top of this. Decorate with a mint leaf and crushed cocoa beans. Serve on a plate, placing 2 brownie squares beside each cappuccino.

This dessert will delight chocaholics. You can substitute walnuts for pecans. Crushed cocoa beans can be bought in shops specializing in confectioners' ingredients and high quality chocolate products.

Grand Marnier and marron frozen soufflé with hot hazelnut frothy topping; chocolate-coated coffee ice-cream lollies

For the frozen soufflé
500 ml (18 fl oz) whipping cream
50 g (2 oz) caster sugar + 200 g (7 oz) caster or granulated sugar for the sugar syrup
200 g (7 oz) raw egg whites (approximately 7 egg whites)
250 g (9 oz) unsweetened sweet chestnut puree (paste)
50 ml (2 fl oz) Grand Marnier

For the hot hazelnut frothy topping
50 g (2 oz) caster sugar
65 g (2–2½ oz) hazelnuts
50 ml (2 fl oz) light pouring cream or whipping cream

For the chocolate-coated coffee ice-cream lollies
2½ leaves gelatine
3 tbsps best quality unsweetened cocoa powder
25 g (1 oz) caster sugar
250 ml (9 fl oz) espresso coffee (or strong instant coffee)
400 g (14 oz) Menier chocolat pâtissier (dark cooking chocolate) to coat the ice lollies
small ice lollipop moulds

Decorate with
pure cocoa powder or best drinking chocolate powder

Grand Marnier and marron frozen soufflé

Beat the cream until it is very firm and stands up in peaks. Chill in the refrigerator.

Heat the 200 g (7 oz) caster sugar with 70 ml (2½ fl oz) water in a small, lipped saucepan with a thick base over a moderate heat until it boils; cook until it reaches a temperature of 121 °C (large ball stage). Beat the egg whites stiffly in a very large bowl preferably with a fixed rotary beater. Beat in 50 g (2 oz) caster sugar to make the egg whites even firmer. Add the hot syrup, pouring it in a very thin stream while beating the egg whites continuously. The resulting meringue mixture should be smooth and glossy; it is called Italian meringue. Leave to become completely cold.

Mix the marron puree with the Grand Marnier and then fold carefully into the cold Italian meringue. Fold in the stiffly beaten cream. Spoon an equal amount of this mixture into tall, freezer-proof glass tumblers and freeze.

Hazelnut froth

Heat the sugar in a small, heavy-bottomed saucepan until it melts and caramelizes to a light brown colour. Add the hazelnuts and stir well. Add the cream and bring to the boil. Leave for 30 minutes, to cool to lukewarm; pour into the blender, process at high speed and strain through a fine sieve. Keep hot in the top section of a double boiler or in a bowl, over gently simmering water.

Chocolate-coated coffee ice-cream lollies

Soften the gelatine leaves by soaking them in a bowl of cold water for 5 minutes.

Mix the cocoa powder and the sugar in a heatproof bowl and add the coffee. Add the gelatine and stir. When it has completely dissolved, pour the mixture into small lolly moulds with the sticks already in place; freeze until solid. Melt the chocolate in a heatproof bowl over hot water, unmould the deep-frozen lollies and dip them in it, one by one, returning them to the freezer once coated.

To serve

Take the tumblers out of the freezer. Beat the hazelnut mixture until it is very frothy indeed with a hand-held electric beater. Spoon the froth into the tumblers, sprinkle a little cocoa or drinking chocolate powder on top and serve accompanied by the chocolate-coated ice-cream lollies.

> This dessert makes the most of the sweet chestnut's natural affinity with chocolate and hazelnuts.
> The hazelnut froth adds a wonderfully light topping that begins to melt the feather-light frozen meringue mixture beneath it. This is a dramatic dessert to serve at the end of a meal.

Crunchy chocolate and raspberry nems, vanilla-flavoured mascarpone

To serve 6

For the crunchy fried *nems*
6 spring roll wrappers (see note on p. 168)
2 small punnets of raspberries
1 egg yolk, lightly beaten
1 litre (1¾ pints) light olive oil or sunflower seed oil for frying
icing sugar

For the chocolate cream (ganache)
150 ml (5 fl oz) full-cream milk
150 ml (5 fl oz) single, pouring cream
2 egg yolks
30 g (1 oz) caster sugar
125 g (4 oz) *couverture* (see note at end of method), coarsely chopped

For the mascarpone cream
250 ml (9 fl oz) whipping cream
250 g (9 oz) Italian mascarpone
50 g (2 oz) icing sugar
1 vanilla pod, slit open

For the chocolate cream (ganache) decoration
200 g (7 oz) double cream
200 g (7 oz) dark, sweetened cooking chocolate (e.g. Menier), coarsely chopped

To assemble the dessert
200 ml (7 fl oz) puree of mixed red berry fruit

The chocolate cream (ganache)

Bring the milk and cream slowly to the boil. Remove from the heat. Beat the egg yolks with the sugar until very pale and light; keep beating continuously as you add the hot milk and cream a little at a time. Return to a very low heat and cook while stirring with a wooden spatula until the custard thickens somewhat; do not allow to boil or it will curdle. Use a double boiler if preferred. Remove from the heat, add the chopped chocolate and stir gently as the latter melts, making sure that it blends evenly into the custard. Pour the custard into small tumblers, until they are half full.

The mascarpone cream

Beat the whipping cream stiffly. Mix the mascarpone with the sugar in a fairly large bowl. Use a pointed knife to scrape the sticky seeds from inside the vanilla pod into the sweetened mascarpone. Fold in the beaten cream.

Chocolate cream (ganache)

Bring the cream to the boil, remove it from the heat, add the chocolate, stir gently but thoroughly and leave to cool. Use 2 teaspoons or coffee spoons to shape little 'eggs' or a melon-scoop to shape balls of chocolate cream, to be used as part of the filling for the 'nems'. Chill these in the refrigerator.

Crunchy nems

Heat the oil (light olive oil or sunflower seed oil) to 180 °C.
Cut each spring roll wrapper (125 mm x 125 mm – 5 in x 5 in) in half and wrap each strip (125 mm x 62 mm – 5 in x 2½ in) securely around a few raspberries and one of the little chocolate dumplings, enveloping them completely, rather like little Vietnamese spring rolls or nems; seal the edges of the nem securely together by brushing with beaten egg yolk. Use a frying basket and lower into the very hot oil to fry briefly until they are pale golden brown; drain and dust with sifted icing sugar.

Assembling the dessert

Working quickly, distribute the *nems* evenly between the tumblers containing the chocolate custard, top with some of the vanilla-flavoured mascarpone cream and drizzle a little red berry puree on top. Serve at once.

> Timing is very important when frying these sweet *nems*: they should be a pale golden colour and crisp but the contents inside should not be subjected to much heat. *Couverture* chocolate, sold to confectioners and to restaurants and so on, usually has to be bought in large quantities. Good quality unsweetened dark cooking chocolate can be substituted.

Honeyed aubergine crumble with frothy lemon sorbet

Crumble

Mix together the flour, icing sugar and the ground almonds. Melt the butter and pour it over this mixture. Use the tips of your fingers to carry out a version of 'rubbing in' until the mixture looks like fine breadcrumbs. Chill in the refrigerator.

Honeyed aubergine

Cut the aubergine flesh into dice approximately 1 cm (3/8 in square). Bring the Muscat wine to the boil with the honey. Add the seeds from the split vanilla pod (scraped out with the sharp point of a knife) and the diced aubergine. Cook over a low heat. When the diced aubergine is very tender, add the lemon juice. Set aside.

Frothy lemon sorbet

Make a sugar syrup by heating the sugar and water; when it has boiled, leave it to cool. Add the freshly-opened, effervescent Perrier water to the cold syrup. Add the egg whites and mix them gently with the lemon-flavoured syrup. Freeze in a sorbetière or ice-cream maker.

Caramelized Banyuls wine

Reduce the wine slowly until it reaches a syrupy consistency.

Cooking and serving

Preheat the oven to 180 °C (gas mark 6). You will need 6 flan or tart rings, non-stick if possible, approximately 12 cm (5 in) in diameter; place these on a non-stick baking sheet and pack them three-quarters full with the aubergine mixture. Add an even layer of crumble topping and bake in the oven until lightly browned (approximately 20 minutes). To serve, put a large spatula under each ring and its contents and carefully transfer to a plate; remove the ring. Garnish with an oval or round scoop of sorbet and surround with some of the caramelized Banyuls wine.

> A pudding made with aubergines? Try it! You will discover something novel and delicious. Sweet dishes and confectionary made with aubergines are very popular in the eastern Mediterranean; in Greece tiny whole aubergines cooked in syrup are sometimes served to welcome a visitor, accompanying a drink or coffee.

To serve 6

6 flan or tart rings 12 cm (5 in) in diameter

For the crumble
100 g (3½ oz) plain flour
50 g (scant 2 oz) icing sugar
60 g (2 oz) ground almonds
60 g (2 oz) butter

For the honeyed aubergine
800 g (1¾ lb) aubergine flesh
150 g (5 oz) lavender honey
375 ml (13 fl oz) Muscat de Frontignan (good quality French Muscat grape dessert wine)
1 vanilla pod
juice of 1 lemon

For the frothy sorbet
500 g (1¼ lb) caster sugar
500 ml (18 fl oz) water
325 ml (11 fl oz) Perrier water
juice of 5 lemons
3 egg whites

For the caramelized Banyuls wine
750 ml (scant 1½ pints) Banyuls good quality French dessert wine

Pineapple gaspacho, mint granita, mixed red berries

To serve 6

For the gaspacho
2 medium-sized pineapples
2 litres (3½ pints) water
400 g (14 oz) granulated
sugar
2 vanilla pods
finely grated zest of 1 lime

For the mint granita
500 ml (18 fl oz) water
250 g (9 oz) granulated sugar
bunch of fresh mint
120 ml (4 fl oz) Perrier water

To assemble and garnish
fresh red berry fruits
(raspberries, sliced
strawberries, wild
strawberries)
6 vanilla pods (top quality not
necessary, see note at end of
method)
slices of dried pineapple
frosted mint leaves (see note
at end of method)

For the gaspacho

Peel the pineapples, removing the hard core, and cut the flesh into fairly small pieces; place in a deep bowl. Bring the water to the boil with the sugar, vanilla pods and the grated lime zest. Pour this flavoured sugar syrup all over the pineapple pieces and leave to stand, at cool room temperature, for 12 hours. After this time, drain the pineapple pieces (pour the syrup through a sieve and reserve) and reduce them to a smooth, thick liquid in the blender or food processor; strain through a fairly fine mesh sieve. Mix with sufficient syrup for a drinkable consistency. Chill in the refrigerator.

Mint granita

Bring the water and sugar to the boil, add the mint leaves and leave to infuse for 15 minutes. Strain through a fine mesh conical (*chinois*) sieve into a large jug or lipped mixing bowl; stir in the Perrier water. Pour into a rectangular, freezer-proof container or bowl and freeze until very firm but not rock hard.

To serve

Run the prongs of a fork firmly along the surface of the frozen mint granita, pressing hard and breaking it up into ice crystals. Mix these briefly and gently with the prepared berry fruits. Simply remove the stalk remains from the raspberries and cultivated strawberries; the wild strawberries (*fraises des bois*) come away cleanly from their stalks when picked.

Spoon a heap of the granita and fruit mixture into the centre of 6 deep soup plates and pour the pineapple gaspacho into the plate to surround it; alternatively, serve as shown on facing page.

Decorate with dried vanilla pods (optional), frosted mint leaves and slices of dried pineapple.

We love pineapple – and it shows! Here it makes an appearance as gaspacho, in a sweet version of the soup with lime juice, its ideal foil. The mint granita adds even more freshness. To frost mint leaves, select the best specimens, dip them one by one in stiffly beaten egg white and then dust with caster sugar. Leave, uncovered, for up to 12 hours at room temperature. To keep these leaves crisp, store them in an airtight container. They will provide a handy decorative touch for a range of desserts.

Caramelized apricots, orange-flower water, almonds, orgeat milk sorbet

For the caramelized
apricots
24 firm, fully ripe apricots
50 g (2 oz) unsalted butter
100 g (3½ oz) caster sugar
48 whole, blanched and
peeled almonds
a few drops of pure almond
essence
1 tbsp orange-flower water

For the orgeat milk sorbet
370 ml (12½ fl oz) orgeat
syrup (orange ratafia)
750 ml (1¾ pints) single,
pouring cream
250 ml (9 fl oz) full-cream
milk

To assemble the dessert
coarsely chopped pistachio
nuts
plain popcorn
a few fresh mint leaves

Orgeat milk sorbet

Mix the 3 ingredients in a saucepan and heat slowly until just below boiling point. Leave to cool, then freeze in a sorbetière or ice-cream maker. Place in the ice box of the refrigerator or in the freezer. (Orgeat syrup is available from certain delicatessens and large grocery shops; it is a mixture of orange-flower water, almond milk and sugar.)

Caramelized apricots

Cut the apricots in half along their natural indentations and remove the stones. Heat the butter and sugar together in a very wide, heavy-bottomed frying pan until very pale golden brown; add the apricots and cook them gently in the caramel, turning each half once. When they have heated through completely (but still hold their shape well), add the whole almonds and sprinkle in the almond essence and the orange-flower water. Stir very gently.

To assemble the dessert

Place 8 apricot halves with their flavoured caramel liquid and 4 almonds in the centre of 6 flat plates; add a scoop of orgeat milk sorbet. Decorate if wished with coarsely chopped pistachio nuts, plain popcorn and a few mint leaves.

Take care when turning the apricots as they heat through, barely cooking in the caramel, to avoid breaking them up at all or damaging their appearance. This dessert is the essence of Mediterranean flavour and delicacy; the better the apricots you use, the more successful the dish.

Strawberry fruit salad in its own syrup, vanilla mini-baba, vanilla ice cream

To serve 5

Strawberry syrup

Place the strawberries and sugar in the top of a double boiler over very gently simmering water and leave to heat through, rather than cook, for 45 minutes. A good deal of juice will be released, forming a light syrup; strain the strawberries in a non-metallic fine mesh sieve. Do not press down on the fruit to extract more juice or the syrup will not be crystal clear. Allow to cool and then chill in the refrigerator.

Sweet yeast dough for the babas

Dissolve the fresh yeast or the dried yeast in 3 tablespoons of warm (not hot) milk and leave it to stand for 5 minutes while the yeast (re)activates. Mix the sifted flour, the dissolved yeast, the butter, salt and honey in the large bowl of a traditional food processor; attach the dough hook and process briefly; when homogeneous, add the eggs one by one, mixing in each egg thoroughly. The dough should be smooth and elastic and should leave the sides of the bowl cleanly; it should not be stiff. Leave to stand for 20 minutes.

Use the extra butter to grease some little Savarin moulds, dariole moulds or similar, small fairly deep cake tins. You will need at least 10 moulds or tins. Break off pieces of the dough and place in the moulds or tins (they should be less than two-thirds full at this point). Leave in a warm, draught-free place to rise for approximately 1 hour; when the dough has risen to fill the moulds, it is ready to bake. Have the oven preheated to 180 °C (gas mark 6). Bake the babas for approximately 15 minutes: they should be well risen and golden brown. Take them out of the oven, turn them out of their moulds and leave to cool completely on a cake rack.

Soaking syrup for the babas

Bring the water and sugar to the boil. Slit the vanilla pod down its entire length and scrape out all the tiny, sticky seeds from inside with the sharp point of a knife; add these to the boiling syrup. Turn off the heat and leave to stand until completely cold. Dip the baba cakes in this syrup, immersing them completely to make sure they are soaked through.

Strawberry fruit salad

Rinse the strawberries briefly and hull them. Cut in half or in quarters, depending upon their size. Mix them gently with the shredded mint.

Assembling the dessert

Heap up the strawberries in mounds in fairly deep plates. Pour the strawberry syrup over them. On each plate place 2 syrup-soaked babas and a neatly rounded scoop of vanilla ice cream.

> Choose the most highly scented strawberries you can find, preferably freshly picked home grown or locally picked ones in season. Wild strawberries (*fraises des bois*) are probably the best but their season is short. Do not refrigerate strawberries: this tends to make them lose their scent and flavour.

For the strawberry fruit salad

750 g (generous 1½ lb) small, very fresh, ripe strawberries
1 small bunch fresh mint, snipped into thin strips

For the strawberry syrup

500 g (generous 1 lb) very fresh, ripe strawberries
75 g (2½–3 oz) caster sugar

For the sweet yeast baba dough

20 g (scant 1 oz) fresh yeast or 10g (2 teaspoons) dried yeast
3 tbsps warm milk
200 g (7 oz) sifted white plain flour
70 g (2½ oz) butter, softened at room temperature + 1 tbsp extra for greasing the moulds
generous pinch of salt
8 g (scant 1 teaspoon) clear, runny honey
5 whole eggs

For the vanilla syrup

500 ml (18 fl oz) water
150 g (5 oz) granulated or caster sugar
1 vanilla pod

Serve with

approximately 450 g (1 lb) best quality vanilla ice cream

Vanilla crème brulée, mascarpone ice cream, fresh strawberry juice

For the crème brulée
16 egg yolks
300 g (11 oz) caster sugar
500 ml (18 fl oz) full-cream milk
250 ml (9 fl oz) single, pouring cream
2 vanilla pods

For the fresh strawberry juice
1 kg (2¼ lb) very fresh, ripe strawberries
150 g (5 oz) caster sugar

For the mascarpone ice cream
1 litre (1¾ pints) full-cream milk
10 egg yolks
250 g (9 oz) caster sugar
300 g (11 oz) Italian mascarpone
250 ml (9 fl oz) crème fraîche, preferably not very thick

For the topping
Cassonade (raw brown cane sugar)

Crème brulée

The day before you plan to serve this dessert, mix all the ingredients listed together (without heating any of them) as follows: beat the egg yolks with the caster sugar until very pale; the mixture should form an unbroken ribbon when the whisk is lifted above it. Add the milk, cream and the vanilla pods (having first slit them lengthwise and scraped the seeds out into the mixture). Chill in a cold larder or in the refrigerator, protected from any strong odours, to allow the vanilla to flavour and scent the mixture for 24 hours.

When this time has passed, preheat the oven to 90 ºC (gas mark 3). Pour the mixture through a very fine mesh sieve (a conical chinois if you have one) into a large jug and fill 10 porcelain ramekins up their inner grooves or 'lips', just under 1 cm (¼ in) below the rim. Cook in the oven for approximately 1 hour or until the custard mixture has set firmly. Allow to cool and then chill in the refrigerator.

Fresh strawberry juice

Place the prepared strawberries with the sugar in the top of a double boiler, over gently simmering water. Cover and heat for 45 minutes. Strain through a fine mesh non-metallic sieve; do not press down on the strawberries to extract extra liquid or the juice will be cloudy. Allow to cool and then chill in the refrigerator.

Mascarpone ice cream

Pour the milk into a large saucepan and slowly heat to just below boiling point. Beat the egg yolks and the sugar until very pale and fluffy (to the 'ribbon' stage, see above). Gradually add the milk in a thin stream while beating continuously. Cook in a heavy-bottomed saucepan over a low heat or use a large double boiler and stir with a spatula as the custard gradually thickens. Do not allow to boil at any point. Remove from heat. Stir in the mascarpone, mixing well. Leave to stand until cold, stirring at intervals, then process in an ice-cream maker.

Make sure you take this ice cream out of the freezer 1 hour before serving it and leave it to stand at cool room temperature. Beat the crème fraîche until it is as frothy as a milk shake; it should not be stiff; fold it into the mascarpone ice cream just before serving.

Assembling the dessert

Sprinkle the cassonade (raw brown cane sugar) evenly over the surface of the chilled ramekins of custard and place them under a very hot grill to caramelize just before serving. Suggested presentation: place a crème brulée on a square plate, place a ramekin of mascarpone ice cream beside it and stand a small, narrow tumbler or liqueur glass of the strawberry juice on the same plate.

This dessert pays tribute to the velvety sweetness of the mascarpone (fresh Italian cream cheese) and the vanilla, accentuated by the fruitiness of the strawberry juice. Most of the preparatory stages can be completed in advance, making it a relatively easy dessert to serve.

Crab and clam croquettes with fresh chilli sauce

To serve 4

For the sauce
1 onion
1 garlic clove
1 tomato
1 lime
1 fresh chilli pepper
100 ml (3½ fl oz) olive oil
juice of 1 lime
pinch of ground cumin
a few fennel seeds, lightly crushed
small bunch fresh coriander
salt

For the croquettes
150 g (5 oz) plain flour
10 g (scant ½ oz – scant 1 tbsp) baking powder
125 ml (4 fl oz) full-cream milk
200 g (7 oz) white crab meat
100 g (3½ oz) fresh golden carpet shell clams (shelled weight) or drained tinned clams
1 small onion, finely chopped
2 large spring onions
2 small garlic cloves, crushed
1 fresh chilli pepper, finely chopped
salt

For cooking and assembling the dish
1 litre (1¾ pints) peanut oil for frying
12 fresh coriander leaves
wooden skewers or satay sticks (optional)
salt

first courses

The sauce

The day before you plan to serve this dish, prepare the sauce: peel and chop the onion finely; crush the garlic clove; blanch, peel and de-seed the tomato, cut the flesh into small dice. Peel off all the pith, peel and membrane from the lime, making it easy to extract the segments from the remaining membrane; cut these segments into small dice. Remove the remains of stalk and the seeds from the chilli pepper and chop the rest very finely. As you prepare all these ingredients, place them in a bowl and then add the remaining ingredients, except the fresh coriander. Cover tightly and leave to stand overnight for the flavours to develop.

The croquettes

The next day, when it is time to prepare and cook the croquettes, sift the flour with the baking powder into a large bowl and mix with sufficient milk until you have a batter that is thicker than you would make for pancakes: it must be thick enough to bind all the additional ingredients you are about to add, and hold them together as they fry. Add the crab flesh, clams (use tinned, well-drained small clams if necessary) and the remaining ingredients, adding the salt to taste. If the batter is not thick enough, stir in a very little additional sifted flour.

Cooking and serving

Heat the frying oil to 180 ºC. Take a heaped coffee spoon of the crab mixture and push this little portion of mixture off the spoon with a fingertip, allowing it to fall into hot oil. Do likewise with the remaining mixture, removing the croquettes from the oil with a slotted spoon when they are browned all over; finish draining them briefly on kitchen paper, sprinkle with a little salt and serve at once, accompanied by the chilli sauce (to which the snipped fresh coriander leaves should be added at the last minute). Decorate with the extra 12 coriander leaves.

How do you choose which types of chilli pepper to use? Shops specializing in Asian and Far Eastern vegetables usually stock a variety, in all sorts of shapes, sizes and colours. We like to use the fresh Thai or Vietnamese red or green chillis, thin and elongated and ranging from 4–6 cm (1½ –2½ in) in length. To prepare these, slit them from top to bottom and remove the seeds with the tip of a small knife. Cut away any pale parts and remains of the stalk before chopping the chilli very finely. Don't touch your eyes or mouth while you are chopping chillis or immediately afterwards! Wash your hands very thoroughly. Some cooks wear disposable gloves when preparing chillis...

Crunchy tuna-filled nori rolls, green pawpaw salad, sesame, water-melon and wasabi sauce

For the tuna rolls

400 g (14 oz) very fresh red tuna fillet

2 Japanese *nori* seaweed sheets (see note at end of recipe)

1 litre (1¾ pints) oil for frying salt

For the green pawpaw salad

1 large green pawpaw

3 tbsps best quality sesame seed oil

1 tbsp rice wine vinegar

pinch of toasted sesame seeds

For the sesame, water-melon and wasabi sauce

1 large piece of fresh water melon, seeds removed, peeled

1 scant tsp commercially prepared wasabi (see note at end of recipe)

For the tempura batter

125 g (4 oz) plain flour

1 egg yolk

pinch of salt

125 g (4 fl oz) iced water

2–3 small ice cubes

Tuna and nori rolls

Cut the tuna fillet into strips about 8 cm (3 in) long, 2 cm (¾ in) wide and 2 cm (¾ in) thick. Cut out strips from the sheets of nori to the same length as the tuna pieces and wide enough to wrap around the tuna fillet, with a little extra for the overlap to secure the roll, leaving the tuna visible only at both ends. Roll up the tuna pieces tightly in the nori wrappers and press the two long edges over each other securely. Make 3 tuna rolls for each refrigerate.

Green papaya salad

Peel the papaya and scoop out all its seeds. Slice it very finely, using a mandoline or a julienne strip cutter. Cover with a damp cloth and chill in the refrigerator. Mix the sesame seed oil and the rice vinegar and dress the papaya with this, adding the pinch of sesame seeds; return the bowl to the refrigerator.

Water melon wasabi sauce

Extract the juice from the water melon with a juicer and cook over a moderate heat until it has reduced to half its original volume and acquired a syrupy consistency. Stir in the spoonful of wasabi and chill in the refrigerator.

Tempura batter

Sift the flour into a large bowl, make a well in the middle and into it put the egg, salt and iced water. Mix until the batter acquires the consistency of a fairly liquid pancake batter. Add the ice cubes.

Cooking and serving

Heat the oil to 180 ºC ready for frying. Pop the tuna and *nori* rolls briefly one by one in the *tempura* batter, drain slightly and immediately add to the frying oil. When the batter turns a pale golden brown remove them from the oil; drain on kitchen paper and sprinkle with salt. Serve the tuna rolls on large flat plates with the green pawpaw salad and the water-melon and wasabi sauce, or use the presentation shown on the facing page.

This recipe has drawn on more than one source for its inspiration: Japan for the tempura; Thailand for the green pawpaw salad. Green pawpaws are usually available in good supermarkets, specialist greengrocers and in shops selling Far-Eastern foods. Choose a sound, firm, completely green fruit. *Nori* is made from dried reddish laver seaweed leaves and is normally used to wrap many varieties of sushi. Wasabi is a pale green horseradish relish, very hot on the tongue and highly flavoured. It is available ready to use in tubes or as powder: all the latter needs is the addition of a few drops of water to form a thick paste and to be left for its distinctive aroma to develop. It is absolutely vital for the *tempura* batter to be kept icy cold until it is used if it is to have the delectable, airy, crunchiness that makes it such a favourite.

Prawns in tempura batter, fried plantains, sweet chilli sauce

16 medium-sized
Mediterranean prawns,
freshly peeled (see note in
method)
oil for frying
salt

For the tempura batter
approximately 100 ml
(3½ fl oz) iced water
2 tbsps plain flour
1 egg yolk
1 ice cube
salt

For the plantain fritters
2 ripe plantain bananas
1 litre (1¾ pints) peanut oil for
frying
salt

For the sweet chilli sauce
4 fresh red chilli peppers
50 g (2 oz) caster sugar
juice of 1 lime
12 fresh coriander leaves
salt

Tempura batter

Mix the iced water, flour and the salt. Beat in the egg yolk last of all. The resulting mixture should be a smooth batter that can be poured but is better described as a thick pancake batter. Chill the batter, having added the ice cube to it, to keep it very cold.

Sweet chilli sauce

Slit the chilli peppers in half (discarding the seeds) and blanch them briefly several times in boiling water, allowing them to cool between each immersion. Cut them into small pieces and place in a small saucepan with the sugar and 200 ml (7 fl oz) water. Boil very gently indeed for as long as it takes for the contents of the pan to acquire a syrupy consistency. Leave to cool, then add the lime juice and the snipped or shredded coriander leaves. Add a little salt.

Frying the prawns in the tempura batter

Heat the frying oil to a temperature of 180 °C. Dip the prawns in the batter and immediately add them to the hot oil; fry them until they are pale golden brown. As soon as they are ready, remove them with a slotted spoon and drain on kitchen towels. Sprinkle with a little salt, if wished. Keep hot.

Plantain fritters

Peel the plantains and cut them into large, chip-shaped pieces. Cook them in the very hot oil until they are crisp and golden brown (they take less time to cook than potato chips). Finish draining on kitchen paper towels and sprinkle with salt.

To serve

Select an equal number of prawns fried in tempura batter and plantain chips – one quarter of the total, and put these on each person's heated plate. Hand round the sauce separately, or serve in individual receptacles.

Tempura batter must be icy cold and has to be fried in very hot oil: this is what gives it a delectable, delicate crispness and crunchiness. Choose ripe plantains, recognizable by their dark brown skins, blotched with black. If you can find only slightly under-ripe specimens, ripen them up in a warm kitchen for a few days. If large pink Mediterranean prawns are unavailable, buy 32 of the best unpeeled Norwegian prawns as they are much smaller, and peel them yourself.

Tastes of the Orient and colours of Asia

Oyster tartare, passion fruit topping, brochettes of sole with gomasio

For the sole brochettes
1 very fresh, large sole fillet
4 wooden skewers or satay sticks
olive oil

For the gomasio
100 g (3½ oz) toasted sesame seeds
very good quality coarse salt
(*fleur de sel*, Maldon)

For the oyster tartare
8 absolutely fresh, live oysters, freshly opened and taken off the shell
scant 1 tsp of finely chopped chives
1 tomato, blanched, skinned, de-seeded and finely diced (see method on p. 48)
1 tbsp olive oil

For the passion fruit sauce
2 large ripe passion fruits
2 tbsps fish stock
5 tbsps olive oil
salt, freshly ground white pepper

Sole brochettes
Slice the fillet of sole lengthwise into 4 strips of even width; thread each of these on to a satay stick or wooden skewer.

Gomasio
Mix the sesame seeds and the coarse salt together, crushing them together lightly (to release the seeds' flavour and help them adhere to the pieces of sole fillet).

Oyster tartare
Chop the oysters coarsely. Mix them in a bowl with the chives, diced tomato and the olive oil.

Passion fruit sauce
Cut each passion fruit in half (you may need to have several fruits in reserve as some imported into this country contain very little flesh and juice) and use a sharp-edged teaspoon to scrape out all the contents into a blender. Add the olive oil, the fish stock (this can be made with the trimmings from the sole; small plastic pots of fish fumet are also available in good supermarkets), and some salt and freshly ground white pepper. Blend very thoroughly at high speed.

Cooking and assembling the dish
Heat a little olive oil in a wide non-stick frying pan; cook the sole brochettes briefly over a high heat, turning them once or twice. Once they are cooked, roll them in the *gomasio* (have this ready spread out on a large plate). Choose 4 fairly large stemmed glasses or tumblers and into each spoon one-quarter of the oyster tartare, top with some passion fruit sauce and then place the sole brochette on top.

Gomasio is one of the simplest Japanese condiments to prepare: it consists of a mixture of toasted white sesame seeds and excellent coarse sea salt. Buy the best coarse salt you can afford for this seasoning, *fleur de sel* from the Atlantic coast, or Maldon from the North Sea coast are both rich in minerals and trace elements and go very well with the nutty sesame seed flavour. Passion fruit pulp has seeds in it that are tough but digestible; you may prefer to push the pulp through a fairly coarse-mesh sieve to get rid of them.

Salmon tataki, peanut sauce, crunchy asparagus spears

To serve 4

For the salmon *tataki*
400 g (14 oz) salmon fillet, cut
from the centre of the fish
2 tbsps olive oil

For the asparagus
16 large, green very fresh
asparagus spears
1 litre (1¾ pints) oil for frying
tempura batter (see recipe on
p.128)
coarse salt, table salt

For the caramelized
balsamic vinegar
500 ml (18 fl oz) balsamic
vinegar

For the peanut sauce
100 g (3½ oz) peanut butter
100 ml (3½ fl oz) water
salt, freshly ground pepper

For the lemon vinaigrette
juice of ½ lemon
3 tbsps olive oil
salt, freshly ground pepper

For the gomasio
2 tbsps toasted sesame
seeds
1 scant tsp best quality
coarse salt

Salmon tataki

Slice the salmon fillet into 2 equal halves. Heat the olive oil in a non-stick frying pan, and when it is very hot sear the salmon pieces on both sides: they should be sealed on the surface, but not cooked inside. Refresh the pieces of salmon immediately by adding them to a bowl of iced water. When they are cold, place them on a clean cloth and dry them well. Place a large piece of plastic food wrap on the work surface. Place the first salmon piece flat on a piece of the food wrap and roll it up tightly, wrap and all, as if you were rolling up a Swiss roll. Secure both sides and tuck excess plastic wrap underneath the rolled up fish. Prepare the other piece of salmon in the same way. Chill in the refrigerator.

The asparagus

Peel, trim and wash the asparagus; tie 12 spears into a neat bundle. Bring plenty of salted water to the boil in a large saucepan; cook the bundle of asparagus until tender but still crisp. Refresh the spears in a bowl of iced water, untie them and spread them out on kitchen paper to drain. Chill in the refrigerator.

Caramelized balsamic vinegar

Reduce the balsamic vinegar over a moderate heat in an uncovered, thick-based saucepan until it acquires a syrupy consistency. Care must be taken during the later stages or it may burn: if the syrup coats the bottom of the pan lightly when it is tipped to one side, it is ready.

Peanut sauce

Mix the water with the peanut butter. Season with salt and pepper and set aside.

Lemon vinaigrette

Mix all the ingredients.

Gomasio

Combine the sesame seeds with the coarse salt. (See note on page 126.)

Frying the asparagus

Heat the oil for frying to 180 °C. Mix all the ingredients for the tempura batter. Dip the asparagus spears one by one in the batter and immediately add the batter-coated spears to the hot oil. Take them out when the batter is crisp and pale golden in colour. Finish draining on kitchen paper and sprinkle with a little salt.

Assembling and serving the dish

Peel the remaining 4 asparagus spears and slice them into long, very thin strips using a mandoline or a very sharp knife. Dress them with the lemon vinaigrette.
Take the salmon rolls out of the refrigerator: cut them into neat slices and carefully remove the wrap from each slice.
Arrange 3 batter-coated asparagus spears on each plate, cover these with slices of the salmon *tataki* and sprinkle with *gomasio*. Top with some of the raw, finely sliced asparagus. Surround with the peanut sauce and a trickle of caramelized balsamic vinegar.

> To make a success out of this version of a Japanese dish, traditionally prepared with fillet of beef, choose only the freshest and best wild salmon (or very fresh tuna) and the freshest asparagus. Remember to have the tempura batter icy cold to ensure that it is very crisp and tender when cooked.

Crisp lobster spring rolls with avocado, tomato and coriander salsa

Lobster spring rolls

Add all the ingredients listed for the court-bouillon to 1½ litres (generous 2½ pints) water. Bring to the boil and continue boiling for 10 minutes, then plunge the lobsters into the pan, allowing them to cook for only 3–4 minutes, depending on their size. Remove and plunge them immediately into a large bowl of iced water. Cut them lengthwise in half along the middle of their backs with a sharp, heavy knife and remove their tails from the shells. Extract all the meat from the claws and large front 'legs'. Cut each piece of the tail meat into 4 or 5 large pieces. Set aside with the claw meat. Cut the spring roll wrappers into rectangles measuring 8 x 4 cm (3 x 1½ in); cut out as many rectangles as you have pieces of lobster to wrap. Spread the spring roll pieces out on the work surface. On each one place the following: 1 tomato 'petal', a pinch of chives, 1 piece of lobster, then season with salt and pepper and roll up just as you would for a spring roll; secure the one free flap to the roll by threading a toothpick through them both, to keep each spring roll closed when it is fried.

Avocado, tomato and coriander salsa

Slice the avocados in half, removing their stones; scoop out the flesh into a bowl and mash them well with a fork, adding the lime juice, chopped spring onion and a little salt. Prepare the tomatoes: blanch for a few seconds in boiling water, refresh in cold water at once, peel and quarter them; take out all the central sections and the seeds, leaving only 4 'petal'-shaped pieces of their outer flesh. Cut these into little dice and add to the avocado mixture. Discard the seeds from the fresh chilli pepper, chop the red flesh and stir into the salsa. Add the coriander and a little more salt.

Cooking and serving

Heat the oil for frying to a temperature of 180 °C. Fry the lobster spring rolls for a few minutes, until they are crisp and golden brown; finish draining them on kitchen paper. Wrap the lobster spring rolls in small cloth napkins or paper serviettes and place on the individual plates, with some of the avocado and chilli salsa in a small bowl beside them. The crunchy spring rolls are dipped into the fresh yet peppery salsa before taking a bite.

> This avocado salsa is a version of Mexican guacamole, at one and the same time a sauce and a salad which is deliciously refreshing. In common with traditional guacamole, the salsa should not be too smooth. Cut the avocados in half, working around the central stone, twist to separate the two halves and use the point of the knife (carefully!) to spear the stone and remove it. Using a fork, crush the flesh while it is still in the skin (some avocado skins are too thin for this treatment) and then scoop all the flesh into a bowl. Prepared this way, the flesh still has some texture to it and is more interesting that way. Get rid of the chilli seeds unless you like extremely fiery tastes – and always wash your hands thoroughly before touching your eyes when you have chopped or touched chillis.

For the lobster spring rolls
4 lobsters, each weighing approximately 450 g (1 lb)
10 spring roll wrappers (see note on p. 162)
32 slow-baked tomato 'petals' (see recipe on p. 60)
1 bunch of chives, finely snipped or chopped
1 litre (1¾ pints) oil for frying
1 packet of tooth picks
salt, freshly ground pepper

For the court-bouillon
1 carrot, sliced into rounds
1 onion, sliced
green section of 1 leek, sliced
1 celery stalk, sliced
1 bouquet garni: 1 bay leaf, sprig of fresh thyme
coarse salt

For the avocado salsa
4 ripe avocados
1 large spring onion or 1 fresh mild white onion
juice of 1 lime
2 bright red, ripe tomatoes
2 fresh chillis
leaves from a small bunch of fresh coriander, snipped or coarsely chopped
salt

129

Tastes of the Orient and colours of Asia

fish and seafood

Grilled langoustine tails with Thai red curry, braised bok choy, coconut milk soup

For the langoustines with red curry
4 large, very fresh raw langoustines
1 tbsp Thai red curry paste (see note at end of method)
1 tbsp olive oil
4 bamboo satay sticks or similar
salt

For the braised bok choy
4 heads of bok choy (see note on p. 22)
20 g (scant 1 oz) butter
1 large spring onion or fresh, mild white onion, thinly sliced
salt, freshly ground pepper

For the coconut milk soup
1 shallot, peeled and very thinly sliced
1 tbsp olive oil
2½ cm (1 in) length of fresh galingale root, peeled
2½ cm (1 in) piece of fresh ginger, peeled
small tin of coconut milk, unsweetened
juice of ½ lime
a few fresh coriander leaves
salt

For the fried apple relish
2 Granny Smith apples
20 g (scant 1 oz) butter
salt, freshly ground pepper

Langoustines with Thai red curry paste

Peel the langoustines (see note on page 83) after you have removed their heads, leaving the tail flippers intact and attached. Reserve the heads and shells for the stock. Impale each langoustine tail on a bamboo satay stick. Mix the Thai red curry paste with a very little water and the olive oil; spoon this all over the langoustines on their sticks and leave them in a cool place to soak up the flavours for 1 hour. Place the heads and shells of the langoustines in a saucepan, add enough water to cover them and boil over a moderate heat for 20 minutes, then strain the stock into a jug through a fine mesh sieve pressing down hard to extract the juice and flavour. Return to the saucepan and boil gently until reduced to half its original volume. Set aside.

Braised bok choy

Trim the bok choy, wash well, and cut each separate stem and its leaf into wide strips. Heat the butter in a thick-based saucepan, fry the bok choy and the spring onion over a moderate heat; add a little water and simmer for 10 minutes. Season to taste and keep hot.

Coconut milk soup

Cook the shallot over a very gentle heat in the olive oil; when it is soft, add the langoustine stock, the galangale and the ginger. Simmer over a low heat for 15 minutes to enable the galangale and ginger to flavour the mixture. Do not allow to boil once you have added the coconut milk, together with the lime juice. Taste and add more seasoning if wished. Remove from the heat and add the coriander leaves at the last minute.

Apple relish

Cut the apples into very thin slices, then cut across these in turn, to produce little matchstick pieces (julienne strips). Fry these in a very little butter over a high heat very briefly; the apple strips should retain some of their crispness. Season with salt and pepper.

Cooking and presentation

Fry the langoustines very briefly in a non-stick frying pan over a high heat; they taste much better if they are slightly undercooked. Sprinkle with a little salt.

Allocate 3 little serving pots for each person: one for the langoustine-flavoured coconut soup; one for the apple relish and one for the braised bok choy. Stand them on large plates with a curried langoustine brochette on each.

Thai red curry paste is very widely sold nowadays, no longer confined to Far-Eastern specialist food shops. It is very hot, with plenty of chillis, so you may choose to taste it before using some for the first time.

Adventures in faraway places:
The French East Indies Company

La Compagnie Française des Indes Orientales (The French East Indies Company) was our main source of inspiration when planning the first Compagnie des Comptoirs. Memories of this seafaring enterprise are evoked by the soft patina of tropical woods, nautical charts on the walls and the subtle impression of setting out on a voyage. The old, four-leaved Afghan door is no mere entrance; it marks the threshold of a world in which we can realize our dreams.

It begins with a poetic succession of names: Yanaon, Mahe, Pondicherry, Karikal, Chandanagore, Surat – the French trading posts in India. These can be accompanied, in their sheer musicality, by the names Goa, Cochin, Calicut, Ceylon; other trading posts that were originally Portuguese but

Above: *a multicoloured array of vegetables arranged with great care, in a market in south India.*
Facing page, left: *the antique Afghan door leading into La Compagnie des Comptoirs in Montpellier.*

which became Dutch. Spices were sought after not only as aromatics and flavourings but for their antiseptic and preservative properties. Cardamom, galangale, ginger, nutmeg, long pepper, chilli pepper and other varieties of capsicum, cinnamon, fenugreek, cloves, turmeric, saffron and, above all, black pepper: this coveted merchandise excited fierce competition and even caused wars. The history of the trading posts was essentially a race for the largest possible share in the spice trade.

The spice race

The Portuguese and Spanish founded the first colonial trading posts in the late 1400s. From 1588 onwards, however, they lost power to the Dutch. The VOM (*Verenigde Oost-Indische Maatschappij*, United East India Company), established in 1602 was effectively a state unto itself: it could mint coin, raise an army, declare war, negotiate treaties and, of course, trade in spices, ivory and silks which it bought at low prices and sold on at a margin of up to 500 per cent. While England had founded the East India Company in 1600, it was not until 1664 that Colbert formed the Compagnie Française des Indes Orientales; once both these countries had become involved, however, it was not long before more confrontations in a long and hard contest followed.

The activities of the French company concentrated on the islands of the Indian Ocean and India, with its ships trading between the Indian port of Surat and the French ports of Lorient, Bordeaux, Nantes and La Rochelle, as well as the arsenal of Rochefort. Pondicherry, the headquarters of the French trading activities in India, was founded in 1674 on the Coromandel coast (now Tamil Nadu); Chandernagore, in Bengal, on the Ganges delta, followed in 1676. The pepper trade was plied along the Kerala and Malabar coasts, while cinnamon was traded in Ceylon and the cassia, star anise and galangale trade centred on China. In the Maldives, French traders acquireded cowry shells which served as currency in Africa for the purchase of slaves. Slaves were exchanged in the West Indies for cane sugar and rum, which were then bartered to buy more slaves, spices, precious stones and silks.

The taste of India – and a taste for India

During the eighteenth century new trading posts were founded: Mahe in Kerala; Yanaon in Andhra Pradesh, and Karikal in Tamil Nadu. France took possession of more territory and set up protectorates. Treaties were signed with the rajahs: the colonial governors employed Indian personnel who maintained good relations with the princely states' rulers through their courtiers. As was later the case with the British Raj, the colonists developed a taste for the spicy flavours of Indian foods (it was the English who invented curry powder, hitherto unknown in India). The colonists also attended Indian festive events. Marriage between the races became widespread. In 1790, when the French company's activities came to an end, only two wholly French families remained.

Further to the south and in the West Indies (the Caribbean), cultivation of tropical crops was developed. The Ile Bourbon and the Ile de France (now Réunion and Mauritius) produced vanilla and sugar. Meanwhile the Dutch and the English sought every means to destroy French trading posts and to thwart their activities, which at one point involved a blockade of the mouth of the Ganges. Increasingly, commercial activity was forced to shift to the West Indies, with its increasingly important trade in sugar, rum, coffee, chocolate and slaves. France's participation in the East Indies trade declined; in 1763, with the signature of the Treaty of Paris, France ceded to England all her Indian possessions with the exception of only five trading posts. The French Company of the East Indies was to last only another twenty-seven years, although the Comptoirs (trading posts) remained French territories until 1954.

In that year, as the French administrators departed, the new mayor of Chandernagore expressed some nostalgia as he bade them farewell, a fairly rare sentiment in the history of decolonization: 'In the secular history of our two nations, one modern, the other ancient, a new chapter begins… which will no longer be polluted by bitter and rancorous relationships between governors and the governed, a chapter that will grow happier with each passing day because of the kindly and cordial relationships that now exist between our two friendly nations.'

Above: *a spice box.*
Facing page, left: *turmeric rhizomes, more bitter than saffron but even more highly coloured. Turmeric is used in many curries; the most sought-after variety comes from Bengal.*

Clam soup with coconut milk, fresh galangale and turmeric, chorizo

2 kg (4½–4¾ lb) fresh clams in
their shells
1 shallot, finely chopped
10 g (scant ½ oz) fresh ginger
20 g (scant 1 oz) fresh
galangale
5 g (¼ oz) fresh turmeric or
generous pinch turmeric
powder
½ small chilli pepper
2 blanched, peeled, de-
seeded tomatoes (see
method on p. 48)
olive oil
200 ml (7 fl oz) coconut milk
(tinned, unsweetened)

To serve

small bunch fresh coriander
1 chorizo sausage (good
quality, Spanish)
juice of 1 lime
olive oil
salt, freshly ground pepper

Wash the clams extremely well in several changes of cold, fresh water; discard any that do not close when handled; drain them and set aside.

Chop the peeled shallot finely; peel the ginger and grate it finely. Peel the galangale and cut it into wafer-thin slices. Peel the fresh turmeric, if used, and chop it finely. Remove the seeds from the chilli pepper. Snip the coriander leaves and set aside for garnishing the finished dish.

Heat 1 tablespoon of olive oil in a wide, deep, heavy-bottomed saucepan or fireproof/oven-to-table casserole dish and in it cook the shallot gently without allowing it to brown at all; add the ginger, galangale and turmeric. Add all the clams, cover and cook over a moderate heat until they have all opened (this will only take a few minutes); discard any clams that do not open.

Use a slotted ladle to take the clams out of the saucepan; keep them warm. Increase the heat under the cooking juices and clam juice left behind in the pan and add the roughly chopped tomatoes. Cook, uncovered, until the liquid has reduced to half its original volume, add as much of the chilli as you wish and finish by pouring in the coconut milk. Simmer for a few minutes.

Serving

Cut 20 very thin slices from the chorizo sausage. Fry them briefly in a non-stick frying pan over a high heat and drain on kitchen paper. Return the clams to the sauce in the large pan, sprinkle the chopped coriander all over them, followed by the lime juice. Add more seasoning if wished and add the thin slices of fried chorizo last of all. Drizzle a little olive oil around the clams and serve at once. Season to taste.

The association of seafood (clams) with pork (chorizo) owes much to the influence of Spain's culinary tradition – and, with the use of coriander, to Portuguese cooking. Use only the very best, moist chorizo, which will have a wonderful, subtle taste and aroma. The coconut milk has nothing to do with the Iberian pensinsula, but its mildness and velvety texture contribute to the success of this highly flavoured dish.

Gurnard fillet baked in a banana leaf, aubergine and mango, spicy tomato sauce

For the fish parcels
600 g (1¼ lb) gurnard fillets
(see note at end of method)
2 fresh, green banana leaves
4 tbsps olive oil
salt, freshly ground pepper
toothpicks or cocktail sticks

**For the aubergine and
mango compote**
1 aubergine
1 ripe but firm Indian mango
1 tbsp olive oil
salt, freshly ground pepper

**For the spicy, syrupy
tomato sauce**
400 g (14 oz) very ripe
tomatoes
150 g (5 oz) caster sugar
(cane sugar)
1 tbsp tomato puree
a dash of sherry vinegar
½ fresh chilli pepper
(optional)
2 tbsps olive oil
salt, freshly ground pepper

Aubergine and mango compote

Peel the mango and the aubergine and cut both into large dice. Heat the aubergine and the mango in the olive oil in a saucepan over a gentle heat; cover and cook very slowly until they are very soft. Remove the lid. If there is any excess moisture left in the pan, cook until it has evaporated completely. Season with salt and pepper.

Fish parcels

Cut the cleaned and prepared fillets into 4 portions. Heat the banana leaves by holding them some way above a gas burner and move them around to heat evenly; this will soften them. Cut out 4 pieces, each a 20 cm (8 in) square. Spoon a generous tablespoon of the aubergine and mango compote onto the middle of the lower half of each banana leaf square. Place a fish fillet on top of this, sprinkle with a tablespoonful of olive oil and season with salt and pepper.

Fold over the upper half of each square, enclosing the fish and compote, and secure with several toothpicks or cocktail sticks to make a neat parcel. Preheat the oven to 180 °C (gas mark 6).

Spicy tomato sauce

Blanch the tomatoes for a few second in boiling water, peel them, remove the seeds and then chop them roughly. Place the tomatoes and all the other ingredients listed for the sauce in a thick-based saucepan and bring to the boil. Turn down the heat and simmer very gently for 1½ hours. Remove from the heat; puree in the blender and add seasoning if needed. Set aside.

Cooking and assembling the dish

Bake the fish parcels in the oven for 15–20 minutes, depending on the thickness of the fish fillets. Remove the wooden toothpicks and serve, using the banana leaves as plates (on top of ordinary plates), handing round the spiced tomato sauce.

> Gurnard (*Trigla lucerna*, also known as the tub gurnard or tub-fish) is caught off the Mediterranean coastline and is remarkable for its beautiful colouration (rosy red on its back, pectoral fins patterned with blue and green) and for its delicate taste. It is an important ingredient in *bouillabaisse*. It is difficult to buy in the United Kingdom but other gurnards, also members of the triglidae family, are widely caught and sold here.

Fillet of sea bass with lemon grass, stir-fried vegetables, tapioca and ginger

For the sea bass fillets
560 g (1¼ lb) sea bass fillets, de-scaled but not skinned
4 fresh lemon grass stalks
olive oil

For the tapioca and ginger sauce
1 litre (1¾ pints) milk
10 g (scant ½ oz) tapioca
50 g (2 oz) *perles du Japon*
40 g (1½ oz) peeled, finely grated fresh ginger
1 tsp olive oil
salt, freshly ground pepper

For the vegetables
2 tbsps grape seed oil
1 small Chinese cabbage (Chinese leaves), finely sliced
2 heads of bok choy (see note on p. 28) cut into large slices
150 g (5 oz) shitake mushrooms
2 carrots, sliced into very thin rounds
2 mild onions, very finely sliced
40 g (1½ oz) fresh ginger, peeled and finely chopped
1 garlic clove, crushed
small bunch of fresh coriander
salt, freshly ground pepper

Last-minute seasoning
best quality coarse salt, freshly ground Sichuan peppercorns

Sea bass fillets

Cut the sea bass fillet(s) into 4 equal portions, weighing approximately 140 g (5 oz) each. Strip off the outermost layers of the lemon grass and trim the remaining stalk to an equal length and thickness (longer than the fish fillets). Slice each stalk in half, cutting at a very oblique angle to make the cut surface sharp: thread the sharp, newly cut ends diagonally through the fillets, 2 for each fillet (they will cross each other in the centre of the fillet, see facing page).

Tapioca and ginger sauce

Bring the milk to the boil in a heavy-bottomed saucepan; stir in the rest of the ingredients listed under this heading, except the seasoning. Simmer very gently without allowing to boil (approximately 80 °C is the ideal temperature) for 45 minutes, then season with salt and pepper. Set aside and keep warm.

Stir-fried vegetables

Heat the grape seed oil over a high heat in a wok. Add all the prepared vegetables and stir-fry them until they are just tender but still very crisp; season with salt and pepper to taste, remove from the heat and add the coriander leaves.

Cooking the fish and assembling the dish

Heat a very little olive oil in a large, non-stick frying pan over a high heat. Place the fillets in the pan, skin side downwards. Do not turn the fillets until the skin is crisp and brown; cook for about 1 minute after turning. Set aside. Arrange a portion of the stir-fried vegetables in the centre of each plate, place the sea bass fillet on top of them, skin side uppermost, sprinkle with a little coarse salt (*fleur de sel* or Maldon) and give a couple of twists of the peppermill to sprinkle with Sichuan pepper. Surround with the *perles du Japon* and tapioca sauce, flavoured with ginger.

This recipe provides an original way of using tapioca and *perles du Japon*, tender and translucent cereal ingredients that seem to be making a welcome return after years of neglect. You will need to search for the *perles de Japon*, but they are still manufactured in Nantes in France and a specialist grocer or delicatessen may stock them. A tip: ginger is easily peeled by rubbing the sharp edge of a teaspoon against the skin!

Giant prawns, fruit grilled à la plancha, cashew nut and tomato salsa

For the fruits *à la plancha*
1 small pineapple
1 cantaloupe melon
2 Indian mangoes (ripe but firm)
1 tbsp olive oil
salt, freshly ground pepper

For the marinated prawns
8 very large fresh Mediterranean prawns or 8 frozen tiger prawns (thawed)
olive oil
30 g (1 oz) fresh ginger, peeled and crushed
½ chilli pepper, de-seeded and finely chopped
juice of ½ lime
Sechuan peppercorns

For the cashew nut and tomato salsa
juice of 1 lime
250 ml (9 fl oz) olive oil
2 blanched, peeled, de-seeded tomatoes, finely diced
small bunch fresh coriander, finely snipped or coarsely chopped
60 g (2 oz) cashew nuts, toasted and coarsely chopped
salt, freshly ground pepper

Peel the pineapple, remove the tough, central core and cut the flesh into slices 1 cm (½ in) thick. Cut the melon into fairly small sections (see facing page), remove the seeds but do not peel. Do not peel the mangoes; cut the flesh into slices 1 cm (½ in) thick, slicing them away from the clingstone as neatly as possible. Peel the prawns but leave their heads and tail flippers attached. Marinate them in a cool place in a mixture of 2 tablespoons olive oil, the crushed ginger and the chopped fresh chilli.

Cashew nut and tomato salsa
Mix the lime juice with a little table salt and a twist of freshly ground pepper. Add the diced tomatoes (see preparation method on page 54), the coriander leaves and the chopped cashew nuts; mix well.

Grilled fruits *à la plancha*
Cook the prepared fruit on a griddle, or in a ridged non-stick griddle pan with a very little olive oil. Season with salt and pepper when seared and lightly cooked.

Cooking the prawns
Heat a little olive oil in a large, non-stick frying pan over a high heat and fry the prawns briefly, turning them once. When they are cooked, sprinkle them with a little lime juice and some freshly ground Sechuan pepper.

To serve
Arrange a selection of the fruit attractively in the centre of each plate, add 2 prawns and surround with some of the cashew nut and tomato salsa.

Grilling *à la plancha* is an original and delicious way of preparing fruit as one of the constituents of a savoury dish. Cashew nuts are all too often confined to the salted variety, served with drinks. When crushed they are used to thicken and add interest to curries, and to Far-Eastern and Brazilian sauces. In this recipe they add a crunchy texture to the subtly sweet-sour taste of the finished dish.

Belly of pork with allspice, polenta, compote of onions and figs

For the pork belly with allspice

4 pieces of best belly of pork for grilling, each weighing 250 g (1/2 lb)

generous pinch of ground allspice

juice of 1 lime

2 tbsps olive oil (+ 3 extra tbsps for cooking and serving)

best quality coarse salt, freshly ground pepper

For the polenta

500 ml (18 fl oz) milk

40 g (1½ oz) unsalted butter

140 g (5 oz) coarse-grain polenta

40 g (1½ oz) mascarpone

For the compote of onions and figs

4 pre-softened, large dried figs

4 mild white onions

30 g (1 oz) unsalted butter

pinch of caster sugar

100 ml (3½ fl oz) sherry vinegar

2 tbsps olive oil

2 tbsps soy sauce

200 ml (7 fl oz) chicken stock or water (as needed)

salt, freshly ground pepper

Place the pieces of pork belly in a shallow dish and rub the allspice powder well into them; do the same with the lime juice and then with the olive oil. Leave to stand for 30 minutes in a cool place.

Polenta

Pour the milk into a thick-based saucepan, add the butter (cut into small pieces) and bring to the boil. Sprinkle in the polenta while stirring continuously and energetically with a balloon whisk; continue cooking over a gentle heat for 30 minutes. Stir in the mascarpone when the polenta is cooked and keep it hot.

Compote of onions and figs

Slice the figs thinly; peel and trim the onions and cut them into wafer-thin slices. Place a heavy-bottomed saucepan over a low heat, add the butter, followed by the figs and onions. Sprinkle with the sugar, cover and cook gently without allowing the onions to brown at all. When the juice or moisture from the onions has almost completely evaporated, stir in one-third of the sherry vinegar, scraping the bottom of the saucepan with a wooden spatula and continue cooking, uncovered, until the vinegar has totally evaporated. Repeat this process twice, with the remaining two-thirds of the vinegar. Remove from the heat. Transfer the contents of the saucepan to a food processor or large blender, add the olive oil and soy sauce and process until very smooth. Add a little chicken stock or water if the mixture is too thick. Add seasoning to taste; transfer to a dish and keep hot.

Pork belly with allspice

Heat 1 tbsp olive oil in a very wide, non-stick frying pan and fry the pieces of pork belly over a moderate heat for approximately 20 minutes; at the end of this time they should be cooked through and browned on both sides. Sprinkle the pork with coarse salt and freshly ground pepper.

Serving the dish

On each heated plate, place a large, well rounded spoonful of polenta; press down lightly in the centre of this mound with a tablespoon and fill the resulting hollow with onion and fig compote. Place each person's portion of pork belly beside the polenta and surround with a trace of olive oil.

If you are short of time, you can use quick-cooking polenta or even the pre-cooked polenta sold in airtight plastic wrapping; the latter will be much heavier and less fluffy than home-cooked polenta, which should, nevertheless, be thick enough to hold its shape when spooned on to the plates. The belly of pork must be very well cooked and it should not be hurried over too high a heat; allow more time if necessary and check at frequent intervals.

Duck roasted on the bone, spiced date chutney, fluffy oat cakes, wine and passion fruit sauce

Spiced date chutney

Take the stones out of the dates and cut the flesh into small pieces. Chop the onion and cook it in the butter over a gentle heat until it is transparent. Add the dates, followed by salt, pepper and the allspice and the sugar. Cook for a minute or two and then add the vinegar, stirring well. Allow to cook over a low heat until the mixture has thickened to a suitable consistency for chutney. Set aside.

Passion fruit and wine sauce

Cook the shallots very gently in the butter. When they are transparent, add the red wine and boil gently, uncovered, until nearly all the wine has evaporated. Stir in the passion fruit puree, the rich duck stock and the sugar. Boil gently, uncovered, to reduce until the sauce is syrupy and has thickened slightly. Add the butter, cut into pieces, and whisk these into the sauce as they melt. Use a hand-held electric beater to homogenise the sauce and add seasoning to taste.

Fluffy oat cakes

Preheat the oven to 180 ºC (gas mark 6). Heat the milk with the butter until very hot but not quite boiling and stir in the porridge oats. Leave to stand for 20–25 minutes. Separate the egg yolks from the whites; stir the yolks into the porridge. Whisk the egg whites stiffly and combine them gently with the porridge mixture. Season with salt and pepper. Spoon the oat mixture into non-stick dariole moulds, filling them two-thirds full. Bake in the oven until well risen and firm to the touch. Remove from the oven and increase the temperature to 220 ºC (gas mark 7–8).

Cooking the duck and serving

Roast the duck bodies (i.e. minus their legs and wings) in a large, heavy-bottomed fireproof casserole dish, allowing them to cook all over for sufficient time to brown and crisp the skin; the fat underneath the skin should start to melt. When the skin is crisp, turn the ducks so that the breasts are uppermost, return the dish to the oven and continue roasting for 10 minutes. When the ducks are done, take them out of the oven and leave to stand in a warm place for 5–10 minutes before carving. Season with salt and pepper. Carve into long, fairly thick slices. Place a fluffy oat cake on each heated plate, a spoonful of date chutney and slices of duck breast. Surround with the passion fruit sauce and also, if wished, a trickle of very good olive oil.

To make your own rich duck stock, make sure you are given the duck giblets with the birds themselves. Trim the livers, hearts and necks of any fat or discolouration and chop them very coarsely. Fry them gently in a little butter with some sliced carrot and onion until lightly browned. Add 750 ml (1¼ pints) of water and some salt and pepper. Bring to the boil, then simmer gently, uncovered for 1 hour. Pour this stock through a fine-mesh sieve and use it to make the sauce. To save time and trouble, thick passion fruit puree is sometimes available deep-frozen; make sure it is not sweetened. Otherwise follow the method given on page 126 to prepare unsweetened puree of fresh passion fruits.

Chicken satay with two sauces, coconut-flavoured rice parcels

To serve 4

peanut oil

For the chicken satay

250 g (9 oz) minced chicken

fresh turmeric

fresh galangale

1 fresh lemon grass stalk

1 garlic clove, crushed

10 g (scant ½ oz) fresh

ginger, peeled and grated

½ fresh chilli, chopped

20 g (scant 1 oz) jaggery

juice of ½ lime

2 shallots, sliced and fried

For the satay (peanut) sauce

fresh lemon grass stalk

fresh ginger

250 g (9 oz) toasted peanuts

50 g (2 oz) tamarind paste

juice of ½ lime

60 g (2 oz) hot shrimp paste

2 garlic cloves, finely chopped

fresh chilli, finely chopped

250 ml (9 fl oz) soy bean oil

For the pineapple sauce

75 g (21/2 oz) tamarind paste

500 ml (18 fl oz) fresh pineapple

juice

60 g (2 oz) hot shrimp paste

2 shallots, finely chopped

2 garlic cloves, finely chopped

⅛ fresh chilli, finely chopped

250 ml (9 fl oz) soy bean oil

For the rice

150 g (5 oz) Thai rice

125 g (4 oz) tinned coconut milk

I banana leaf

Chicken satay mixture

Chop sufficient fresh turmeric and galangale to yield 1 tablespoon of each. Finely chop the lemon grass. Mix all the ingredients listed for the chicken mixture until homogeneous. Add more seasoning if wished. Take some of the chicken mixture and press it around the satay stick, shaping it into a flattened ball covering about a quarter of each stick.

Two sauces

Satay (peanut) sauce: crush the toasted peanuts; finely chop sufficient lemon grass to yield 2 tablespoonfuls and sufficient ginger to yield 1 tablespoonful. The next stage is similar for both sauces. Dilute the tamarind paste for the pineapple sauce by placing it in a fine-mesh plastic sieve and lower the sieve halfway into a bowl of pineapple juice; stir the tamarind in the sieve with a small wooden spoon until it has completely dissolved. Follow the same procedure with more tamarind paste for the satay sauce but use a fairly small bowl containing the lime juice diluted with cold water. Stir the shrimp paste into these bowls of tamarind solution; add all the remaining ingredients. Stir in table salt according to taste into the sauces. Set aside the two bowls.

Coconut-flavoured rice parcels

Add sufficient cold water to the rice to cover it by 1 cm (⅜ in). Bring to the boil, cover tightly and cook over a very gentle heat until all the water has been absorbed by the rice, which should be tender but still have a little 'bite' left in the grains. Add the coconut milk, cover tightly again, and return to a very gentle heat for 2 minutes; remove from the heat and leave to stand for 10 minutes. Spread the rice out in an even layer in a wide, shallow dish; when cold, add salt to taste and press down again into an even layer.

Heat the banana leaf over a gas burner to soften it. Cut out 4 large squares. Use a palette knife to mark out 4 squares of rice about half the size of the banana leaf squares; lift these 'cakes' of rice onto the banana leaf squares and wrap them up, securing with toothpicks.

Cooking the satay sticks and serving

Preheat the oven to 160 °C (gas mark 5–6). Heat a little peanut oil in a very wide frying pan and fry the satay sticks flat, turning once. Keep hot. Meanwhile reheat the rice packets in the oven. Serve them on plates, together with two small bowls, each containing a little of the two dipping sauces. The satay sticks can be served on the same plate or put into a tumbler, with a wedge of lime if wished.

Jaggery or palm sugar is sold in shops that specialize in Far-Eastern foods, usually in the form of large cakes of unrefined sugar that have to be broken into pieces with a mallet. Asian grocery shops or the larger supermarkets will usually have all the other ingredients, such as tamarind paste, hot shrimp paste, coconut milk, Thai rice, galangale, fresh chillis and fresh turmeric (you can substitute scant 1 teaspoon of turmeric powder for this last ingredient). Banana leaves may prove something of a challenge: try West Indian shops.

Veal chops marinated à l'orientale
with a chinoiserie of linguini and vegetables

To serve 4

4 veal chops, each weighing
approximately 250 g (8–9 oz)
120 g (4 oz) fresh linguini
pasta
olive oil
salt, freshly ground pepper

For the marinade
juice of 1 lime
100 ml (3½ fl oz) soy sauce
scant 1 tsp of clear, runny
honey
small piece of fresh ginger,
peeled and grated
2 tbsps sesame seed oil
½ garlic clove, crushed

**For the mixed julienne
strips of vegetables**
1 carrot
120 g (¼ lb) soy bean sprouts
1 leek
¼ Chinese cabbage
(Chinese leaves)
12 fresh shitake mushrooms
2 large spring onions or fresh
white onions, cut into strips
or sliced into thin rings
small bunch fresh coriander
sesame seed oil
soy sauce
salt, freshly ground pepper

To serve
generous pinch of toasted
sesame seeds

Start preparing this dish a day in advance: mix all the marinade ingredients and marinate the veal chops in a cool place or refrigerator.

The linguini pasta

Shortly before you plan to serve this dish, bring a large saucepan of salted water to the boil, add scant 1 teaspoon of olive oil and cook the linguini until they are just tender but still have a little bite left in them (al dente). Drain and rinse under the cold tap. Drain again.

Julienne of vegetables for the 'chinoiserie'

Peel and trim the vegetables and cut them all into julienne strips except the bean sprouts; leave those as they are except for discarding as many of the bitter little green seed pods as possible.

Cooking the veal chops

Take the chops out of the marinade and wipe them dry with kitchen paper towels. Pour 100–125 ml (3½–4 fl oz) of the marinade into a small saucepan and reduce over a gentle heat. Add seasoning if necessary and keep warm. Fry the chops over a moderate heat, turning them once: they should be lightly browned on the outside, still slightly pink inside. Wrap them in foil and keep warm.

Cooking the vegetables

Heat a little sesame seed oil in a wok or large, non-stick frying pan and stir-fry all the vegetables over a fairly high heat, starting with the carrots: cook these for 1 minute, then add the shitake mushrooms; stir-fry these for 1 minute, then at 1-minute intervals add the leek, followed by the Chinese cabbage, the spring onions and, finally, the bean sprouts. Add the coriander leaves, remove from the heat immediately and sprinkle with a little soy sauce and sesame seed oil. Stir in the linguine, mixing them evenly with the vegetables and return to the heat briefly, stirring and turning, until the linguine have reheated.

To serve

Roll the linguini and the julienne strips of vegetables around a fork and push off the fork onto individual heated plates, to form a 'nest' for the pork chops. Surround with a trickle of the reduced marinade. Sprinkle with toasted sesame seeds.

This Chinese-inspired marinade goes very well with the delicate, tender flesh of veal chops, but they need careful attention while they are frying as the soy sauce and honey tend to make the surface of the chops caramelize and brown much more rapidly. Try to buy the more flavoursome farm-reared veal in preference to the bland and slightly 'soggy' veal from milk-fed crated calves. Thin Chinese wheat noodles (fresh or dried) can be used instead of linguini.

Pork and prawn kebabs and savoury mango salad with herbs

For the kebabs
4 slices, 200 g (7 oz) each, of boned spare rib and/or bladebone cut of pork
4 large prawns, unpeeled
pinch of ground cumin
2 pinches of allspice
2 large spring onions or fresh white onions
peeled, crushed cloves from 2 heads of garlic
1 fresh chilli pepper, de-seeded and finely chopped
½ bunch of fresh coriander
2 tbsps olive oil
salt
8 wooden skewers or satay sticks

154

For the mango salad
2 ripe, firm Indian mangoes
½ fresh chilli pepper, de-seeded and crushed
chopped leaves from a small bunch of fresh coriander
juice of 1 lemon
1 tomato, blanched, peeled (see method on p. 48), de-seeded and diced
2 tbsps olive oil
salt, freshly ground pepper

For the tomato sauce
2 bright red, ripe tomatoes, (see recipe on p. 54)
50 g (2 oz) caster sugar
2 tbsps rice wine vinegar
olive oil
harissa (optional)
salt, freshly ground pepper

Tastes of the Orient and colours of Asia

meat

Kebabs

Peel the prawns, removing their heads and tail flippers. Place them on a large chopping board with the pork. Chop very finely with a very sharp, heavy knife (do not mince). Add the spices, the onions, garlic (cut each clove in half and remove the central shoot if wished), chilli and coriander leaves and, finally, some salt. Mix all these ingredients very thoroughly with your hands, to form a firm mass that sticks together. Divide in half and then in half again; each of these quantities needs to be sub-divided in turn and shaped into 4 very firm balls or oval rissoles, yielding 16 in total. Thread 2 of these on to each skewer or satay stick and squeeze gently to secure.

Savoury mango salad

Peel the mangoes with a very sharp serrated knife and cut off very thin slices. Cut the largest slices in half. Transfer to a bowl and mix with the crushed chilli, coriander leaves, lemon juice and the finely diced tomatoes. Season with salt and pepper and set aside.

Tomato sauce

Crush the ripe tomato flesh. Press the flesh down into a sieve to extract all the juice. Heat the sugar until it forms a caramel and when this has darkened to a light brown colour, add the rice wine vinegar and stir well. Add the tomato juice and reduce over a low heat until the mixture is much thicker and 'syrupy', almost glossy in appearance. Season to taste, add a few drops of olive oil. You may wish to add a very little harissa if you like hot, peppery sauces.

Cooking the kebabs

Heat the olive oil over a high heat in a very wide, non-stick frying pan and fry the kebabs until they are well browned and cooked through (turn them two or three times).

Serving the dish

Place 2 tablespoons of the mango salad on each plate and add 2 pork and prawn kebabs. Hand round the tomato sauce separately in a jug or sauce boat.

Pork and prawns are very frequently combined in Far-Eastern recipes; the Portuguese also love this combination and it is becoming increasingly popular in other western countries. These kebabs are very easy and rewarding to cook. To save time, you can use 200 ml (7 fl oz) good quality commercially prepared tomato juice. Unless you like extremely hot tastes, it is advisable to remove the seeds from the chilli peppers.

Adventures in faraway places: Asia, the Indian Ocean, the Islands

While the décor of Le Jardin des Sens – the Montpellier restaurant of La Compagnie des Comptoirs – draws on the East Indies for its inspiration, our restaurant on the beach at La Grande-Motte, the Effet Mer, evokes even more far-distant destinations. Here, too, there is a great, carved-wood door, admitting the visitor to an atmosphere of dreams and relaxation. The door is not surrounded by walls and it looks out, like the remnants of an ancient ark, over the dunes, towards a wide, horizontal marine landscape. In common with much of the furniture and woodwork, the door has travelled all the way from Bali. The panelling in the restaurant divides its space rhythmically into sections and the panels are decorated with carvings of flowers. Elsewhere, large, antique beds, with draperies hanging from

Above: *the bar at La Compagnie des Comptoirs in Avignon unfolds like a drowned bamboo thicket, with a greenish light glowing between the stems. Facing page, left: the same tropical light filters through a green parasol sheltering the wares of a trader in the floating market in Bangkok.*

Below: *a sugar cane field in Martinique, photographed during the 1920s for the French colonial administration's records.*
Facing page, right: *coconut is an all-purpose ingredient in African, South-American, Indian and Indonesian cooking.*

their frameworks, await only the visitor's presence, ready to dispense repose surrounded by the wind, the sea and the sun. The Moroccan *salon* provides shade, calm and intimacy.

We have brought Morocco and Indonesia together, into the same space, the better to express our love of travel in the widest sense, without ever remaining at a particular destination. What counts is the exoticism, luxury and sensuality associated with everything that is far off, unfamiliar and beautiful.

Harmonious marriages, subtle associations

The dishes we serve are in harmony with this principle, discernible in the ingredients, and in the culinary techniques borrowed from the gastronomic traditions of south-east Asia, China, Japan and the many islands of that vast expanse of the world. Often these different styles share the same plate: a Thai pawpaw salad with *wasabi* (Japanese horseradish); an Afro-American favourite, plantain banana, with tempura; roast duck served with a red wine sauce – and with a date chutney as well; *nems*, the little Vietnamese version of spring rolls, served as a dessert with raspberries inside them

Above: *green pawpaws and mangoes: these two fruits can be eaten before they are ripe; in Asia and in the West Indies they are used when still green, both raw and cooked, to make refreshing salads and as accompaniments to meat and fish dishes.*

and accompanied by Italian mascarpone; Chinese litchis with a Basque liqueur, Izarra. We are not seeking to be provocative with these combinations of various dishes; they are the fruit of a meticulous search for harmony. This is the spirit that informs modern cooking, choosing from an ever-widening selection while trusting to what our senses and our discernment tell us.

Thailand remains one of the favourite sources of inspiration for our cooking. Thai dishes have such finesse, they are so delicately balanced, the variety of ingredients is so vast and such is the subtlety of their tastes that they never cease to surprise us. Thai food exploits a wide range of sensations: the scale goes from extremely peppery – this is one of the world's hottest cuisines – to the soothing mildness provided by coconut milk, peanuts, green papaya and rice. In the Thai repertoire of spices some tastes are as subtle as you will find anywhere: galangale, the leaves of the kaffir lime, lemon grass, the leaves and roots of fresh coriander, complemented by chilli peppers, limes, shrimp paste and the fish sauce that is reminiscent of the ancient Romans' *garum*. We also team crustaceans such as Mediterranean prawns, crabs, and the smaller prawns and shrimps with Thailand's sweet and peppery sauces, or with Thai red, yellow or green curry paste, and adopt the simple yet subtle method of cooking them gently, wrapped in banana leaves.

Japanese cooking is another of our points of reference. Here, the basic materials and foodstuffs make their presence felt more boldly and more simply, in a more straightforward manner. Salmon and tuna are prepared using the *tataki* method, just seared on the surface to seal them and then plunged into iced water to produce a dish that is at one and the same time robust, fresh and light. The essence of this dish consists of the variety and originality of its cooking techniques, in the raw-cooked contrast, with the finishing touch of a full-bodied and aromatic soy sauce and a hint of *wasabi*.

The never-ending journey of the venturesome gourmet

Other dreams lead us to the Islands, those of the Pacific, of the Indian Ocean and the Gulf of Mexico. The expression 'the Islands' was once, and to a certain extent still is, synonymous with a bygone era and, hearing it, French people would immediately think of all those far-off parts of the world where the French traded in spices and cultivated crops in tropical plantations. France used to be heavily involved in trading in pepper from Zanzibar, cinnamon from Sri Lanka and cassia wood from Borneo, cloves from the Moluccas, vanilla from Madagascar, Réunion and Tahiti; allspice from Jamaica, dried orange peel from Haiti and Curaçao. Away from the islands, China was where French merchants traded in star anise and Sichuan pepper; West Africa supplied cardamoms and ginger, cocoa and cashew nuts. As for the countless varieties of capsicums and chilli peppers in every shape, form and strength, coconuts and fresh coriander, these are available throughout the tropics. Exotic fruits create a feast for the eyes and palate on one's plate and give a touch of refinement to desserts. They are always included in our *voyages gourmands*. The mango, which originated in Asia, has spread to most tropical regions and it is a favourite, not only because of the tree's beauty but, more pertinently, for the sensual flavour and aroma of its fruit. Pawpaw is another tropical fruit that is also eaten when green, grated for refreshing salads in the cooking of south-east Asia. When ripe the flesh is delicious sprinkled with lime juice. The pulp inside the passion fruit has a wonderful scent and taste which completely transforms desserts, while the pineapple, which has been known in France since the reign of Louis XIV three hundred years ago, remains one of our favourite fruits: we use it a great deal, in both savoury and sweet dishes.

Above: *little fishing boats on the Pearl River, just off Macao, where for centuries the cooking has mirrored the region's racial diversity, blending the culinary traditions of China and Portugal.*

Adventures in faraway places: Asia, the Indian Ocean, the Islands

Crisp spring rolls with guinea fowl filling, pawpaw salad with cashew nuts, fresh coriander

To serve 4

**For the crisp spring rolls
with guinea fowl filling**
2 boned thighs of guinea fowl
2 tbsps soy-maple sauce (mix
½ tbsp soy sauce with 1½
tbsps maple syrup)
4 wooden skewers or bamboo
satay sticks
2 spring roll wrappers (see
note at end of method)
1 egg yolk lightly beaten with
1 tsp cold water
1 litre (1¾ pints) oil for frying

For the pawpaw salad
1 under-ripe, firm pawpaw
1 tbsp lemon juice
3 tbsps olive oil
1 shallot, finely chopped
small bunch fresh coriander
salt, freshly ground pepper

Garnish with
1 tbsp toasted, coarsely
chopped cashew nuts

Cut the guinea fowl flesh into large dice; marinate for 20 minutes in the soy sauce and maple syrup mixture. Take the leaves off the coriander stalks and snip them coarsely.

Pawpaw salad

Peel the pawpaw and grate it (do not include any of dark seeds or their surrounding filaments). Season with salt and pepper and mix the grated pawpaw with the lemon juice, olive oil and shallot. Add the coriander shortly before serving.

Crisp spring rolls with guinea fowl filling

Drain off the marinade from the diced guinea fowl meat, pouring it into a small saucepan. Cook gently until it looks like a syrup; set aside.

Cut the spring roll wrappers into rectangles that, when wrapped round the meat section of each brochette, will completely cover it.

Dip the wooden skewers or satay sticks in cold water and then impale an even number of diced guinea fowl pieces on each one. Wrap the pieces of spring roll wrapper fairly tightly around the meat on the skewer; brush the edges and the long 'side seam' of wrapper with beaten egg and press lightly to secure.

Heat the oil until very hot (160 °C) and deep-fry the spring-roll-wrapped brochettes (use a frying basket if wished) until they are golden brown. Remove from the fryer and finish draining on kitchen paper.

To serve

Spoon the pawpaw salad onto small plates or into small bowls, sprinkle with the cashew nuts and place the brochettes on top; alternatively, serve as shown on facing page. Sprinkle each serving with a little of the reduced marinade.

> Spring roll wrappers are sold in all Chinese food shops; sheets of *brick* can be used instead, but do not use the rice flour Vietnamese spring roll (nems) wrappers which have to be moistened before use as they are not suitable for this dish.

Oriental pastry with pears, spiced syrup and quince sorbet

For the quince sorbet
1 litre (1¾ pints) water
600 g (1¼ lb) sugar
500 g (generous 1 lb) cooked
quince flesh

For the spiced syrup
250 ml (9 fl oz) water
150 g (5 oz) sugar
½ vanilla pod
½ cinnamon stick
2 star anise
1 scant tsp Sechuan
peppercorns
1 tbsp potato flour

For the pear pastry
200 g (7 oz) butter, softened
at room temperature
+ 100 g (3½ oz) butter, melted
200 g (7 oz) caster sugar +
50 g (2 oz) for the filo sheets
2 eggs
200 g (7 oz) ground almonds
3 pears
10 sheets of filo pastry (see
note on p. 34)
50 g (2 oz) chopped pistachio
nuts
100 g (3½ oz) chopped
almonds
100 g (3½ oz) clear, runny
honey

To serve
extra spices (for decoration)
fresh mint
icing sugar

Quince sorbet

Make a syrup with the sugar and water: bring them to the boil and, when the sugar has completely dissolved, leave to cool.
Mix the cold, cooked quince flesh and the cold sugar syrup thoroughly; transfer this mixture to a sorbetière or ice-cream maker and freeze. Transfer to the freezer.

Spiced syrup

Mix the water, sugar and the spices in a saucepan; bring to the boil and allow the sugar to dissolve completely. Have the potato flour ready mixed with approximately 2 tablespoons of cold water and stir into the syrup to thicken slightly. Cook while stirring over a very gentle heat for a few minutes. Remove from heat.

Pear pastry

Make the almond filling: beat the softened butter with 200 g (7 oz) caster sugar until pale and fluffy; beat in the eggs one at a time, then stir in the ground almonds. Set aside.
Peel the pears, cut them in half, remove the cores and slice them thinly.
Preheat the oven to 160 ° (gas mark 5–6).
Cut the filo sheets in half across their width; brush all the exposed surfaces with melted butter, using a soft pastry brush; use the extra 50 g (2 oz) of caster sugar to sprinkle over the butter-coated surfaces.
Using a large, non-stick baking sheet or very shallow baking tray that will accommodate the filo sheets lying flat, place 5 of the buttered and sugar-sprinkled filo sheets on it, on top of one another; these layers will only have butter and sugar between them. Spread the egg, sugar and almond mixture over the top layer and smooth it level with a palette knife; place

the sliced pears on top in an even layer and sprinkle them with all the chopped pistachio nuts and half the almonds. Sprinkle as evenly as possible with the honey. Place the remaining filo sheets (brushed with butter and sprinkled with sugar) on top of the almond cream, nut and honey layer. Sprinkle the top evenly with the remaining almonds. Bake for approximately 40 minutes. The surface of the pastry should be an even golden brown.

To serve

Cut the hot pastry into wide parallel strips and then into elongated triangles. Place 3 of these on each person's plate and sprinkle with some of the thickened spiced syrup.
Serve with a scoop of the quince sorbet. Decorate with spices (e.g. star anise), if wished, and with fresh mint leaves; dust lightly with sifted icing sugar.

We have added pears to our variation on the classic technique for baking *baklava*. Fruit adds a welcome fruity and slightly acid touch to the sweet pastry. This dessert combines crispness, melting softness and spiciness; it is much better served warm than cold. Keep the remaining filo sheets well wrapped up in the refrigerator for later use.

'Trading Post' caramelized exotic fruits with spices, piña colada ice cream, Curaçao sauce

For the caramelized exotic fruits
50 g (2 oz) butter
200 g (7 oz) caster sugar
1 small, ripe pineapple
1 ripe pawpaw
1 ripe, firm mango
2 kiwi fruits
2 slightly under-ripe bananas
4 star anise
4 cinnamon sticks
2 vanilla pods
4 saffron pistils (or whole saffron 'threads')
4 twists of freshly milled Sechuan pepper
scant 1 tsp spices for *pain d'épices* (honey spice bread), see note at end of method

For the Curaçao sauce
370 ml (approximately ½ pint) Curaçao liqueur
100 g (31/2 oz) caster sugar

For the piña colada ice cream
10 egg yolks
160 g (generous 5 oz) caster sugar
500 ml (18 fl oz) pineapple pulp (see note at end of method)
500 ml (18 fl oz) tinned coconut milk
100 ml (3½ fl oz) Jamaica rum

Piña colada ice cream

Start preparation the day before you plan to serve this. Beat the egg yolks with the caster sugar until very pale and frothy; the mixture should form a 'ribbon' when the whisk is lifted above the bowl. Bring the pineapple pulp and coconut milk to the boil together in a saucepan, remove from the heat and stir gently into the sugar and egg mixture; return this to the saucepan (or use a large double boiler) and cook over a gentle heat (or over simmering water) until the mixture reaches a temperature of 85 °C (it should just thicken slightly); do not allow it to come close to boiling at any point. Pour into a large, lipped bowl and stir in the rum. Chill in the refrigerator for 24 hours. Process in the ice-cream maker 30 minutes before serving.

'Trading Post' spiced exotic fruits

Peel and prepare all the fruits and cut them into pieces of your preferred size and shape. Heat the butter in a very large, deep saucepan. Add the sugar and the following spices, just as they are, without grinding or crumbling them: star anise, cinnamon sticks and the vanilla pods (which should be slit lengthwise and the seeds and pods both added to the pan); lastly, add the saffron. Add all the fruit and cook over a moderate heat, just long enough for them to heat through and be coated with the light caramel. While they are cooking, sprinkle with the freshly ground Sechuan pepper and *pain d'épices* spice mixture.

Curaçao sauce

Mix the Curaçao and the sugar in a heavy-bottomed saucepan; reduce over a moderate heat until it becomes syrupy. Leave to cool.

Assembling the dessert

Arrange a selection of the warm or cold spiced fruits on each dish. Place a scoop of the piña colada ice cream to one side and drizzle the Curaçao sauce over it; trickle a thin ribbon of the sauce around the serving of fruits as well.

To make your pineapple pulp, simply place the peeled and cored flesh in a food processor or blender and process until smooth. If you have to use tinned pineapple, drain it well beforehand. *Pain d'épices* (spiced honey bread) mixture is blended, using ground spices, as follows: 10 g ground cinnamon, 5 g ground (powdered) ginger, 15 g ground fresh, green (or dried) anise seeds, 5 g ground nutmeg, 5 g ground cloves. Mix well and sprinkle a pinch over each serving. You may prefer to grind the whole spices in a coffee grinder for a fresh mixture. Keep what is left over in an airtight jar. The Sechuan peppercorns must be freshly ground in a pepper mill.

Caramelized pineapple and lemon grass brochettes, exotic fruit and orange-flower water sauce

To serve 4

For the pineapple brochettes
25 g (1oz) dried apricots
25 g (1 oz) seedless raisins
orange-flower water (for soaking the dried fruit)
1 large pineapple, not too ripe
2 lemon grass stalks and bulbs
50 g (2 oz) caster sugar
20 g (scant 1 oz) unsalted butter

For the exotic fruit sauce
75 g (2½ oz) ripe apricot flesh (pureed)
75 g (2½ oz) ripe peach or nectarine flesh (pureed)
200 g (7 oz) fresh passion fruit pulp, sieved, or juice
100 g (3½ oz) unsweetened mango juice (or pureed flesh)
1 vanilla pod (slit to release the seeds)
1 cinnamon stick
2 star anise

Exotic fruit sauce

Place all the fruit and fruit juices in a saucepan with the spices. Bring slowly to the boil. Remove from the heat, cover tightly and leave to stand, for the flavours to develop.

Caramelized pineapple brochettes

Place the apricots and the raisins in a small, deep bowl or cup and add sufficient orange-flower water to cover them completely. Leave to soften and flavour.

Peel and core the pineapple and cut in quarters. Remove the outermost layer of the lemon grass and slice off the very top of the stem at a very slanting angle. Cut the lemon grass lengthwise in half. Thread the chunks of pineapple onto these lemon grass 'skewers', pushing the sharp, freshly cut end in first. Heat the butter and sugar in a wide, non-stick frying pan until the sugar has completely dissolved; add the 'brochettes' of pineapple and cook them over a moderate heat, turning 3 times so that all the exposed surfaces caramelize. As soon as they are golden brown all over, add the exotic fruit juice to the pan and continue cooking, still uncovered, for up to 10 minutes over a gentle heat.

To serve

Transfer to deep dessert plates or bowls and surround with the soaked dried fruits and juices.

> You may wish to add an extra, exotic touch by cooking and/or serving this dish in an earthenware *tajine*, typical of Moroccan cooking. In France *pêches de vigne* (red-fleshed peaches grown among the vines) are used for this recipe. Choose the best quality, plump, moist dried fruits you can buy. The use of lemon grass adds an unexpected Far-Eastern flavour to this dessert. The pineapple should be just ripe; it will soften during cooking.

Poached lychees, granita of Izarra liqueur, iced water flavoured with lemon verbena

For the poached lychees
1 litre (1¾ pints) water
200 g (7 oz) granulated or
caster sugar
20 lychees (peeled and
stoned)

For the Izarra granita
1 litre (1¾ pints) water
600 g (1¼ lb) caster sugar
500 ml (18 fl oz) Perrier water
200 ml (7 fl oz) green Izarra
liqueur

**For the iced water
flavoured with lemon
verbena**
1 litre (1¾ pints) Perrier water
200 g (7 oz) granulated or
caster sugar
small bunch fresh or dried
lemon verbena

For decorating the dessert
A few fresh lemon verbena
leaves
coarsely chopped pistachio
nuts

Poached lychees

Bring the sugar and water to the boil in a saucepan; when the sugar has completely dissolved, add the peeled, stoned lychees and poach them for 5 minutes. Allow to cool; when cold, chill in the refrigerator, in the cooking syrup.

Granita of Izarra liqueur

Mix the sugar and water until the sugar has dissolved completely (do not heat). Stir in all the remaining ingredients and pour into a rectangular freezer-proof container. Place in the freezer. When the time comes to serve the granita, break up the frozen mixture into ice granules by scraping the tines of a strong fork along the surface.

Iced water flavoured with lemon verbena

Bring the Perrier water and the sugar to the boil. Add the lemon verbena, cover and leave to infuse for 15 minutes, away from the heat. Pour through a fine-mesh strainer and, when cool, refrigerate.

To serve

Spoon the granita into glass coupes or small bowls, sprinkle with the lemon verbena iced water. Place the drained lychees on top of the granita and sprinkle with some chopped pistachios. Decorate with a fresh lemon verbena leaf.

In this dessert a Chinese fruit and Izarra liqueur (its taste reminiscent of sage and rosemary, made in the French Pyrenees, in the Basque country) combine their very refreshing tastes, accentuated by the use of lemon verbena. This is an ideal dessert to serve at the end of a rich meal.

Carrot 'ravioli' with lime custard cream filling, vanilla sauce and lemon balm

4 very large, fresh, preferably
organic carrots
200 g (7 oz) caster sugar
500 ml (18 fl oz) water

For the lime custard cream
5 egg yolks
100 g (3½ oz) caster sugar
500 ml (18 fl oz) double
cream
finely grated zest of 2 limes

**For the vanilla and lemon
balm sauce**
200 ml (7 fl oz) water
20 g (scant 1 oz) caster sugar
½ vanilla pod
7 g (approximately 1 tbsp)
potato flour

To serve
shredded fresh lemon balm
leaves

Lime custard cream
The day before you plan to serve this dish, complete this first preparation stage for the lime cream. Beat the egg yolks with the sugar until pale and very creamy; fold in the cream and the grated lime zest. Chill in the refrigerator for 24 hours.

Carrots
These should be prepared on the day the dish is to be served. Peel and trim the carrots; slice them very thinly into rounds, using a mandoline or a very sharp knife. You will only use the large discs of carrot. Bring the water and sugar to the boil, add the carrots and cook them over a gentle heat for 15 minutes. Leave to cool completely.

Vanilla and lemon balm sauce
Bring the water and sugar to the boil with the vanilla pod and its seeds, having first scraped these out into the water. Mix the potato flour with a little cold water and add sufficient to thicken the vanilla-flavoured liquid a little; stir while cooking over a gentle heat for a few minutes. Remove from heat.

Cooking and assembling the dessert
Preheat the oven to 90 °C (gas mark 3). Strain the lime cream through a sieve and pour it into a shallow, non-stick baking tray or ceramic dish. Place the tray or dish into the oven and bake for 1 hour. Remove from the oven and allow to cool.

Drain the carrot slices. Use a very small-diameter pastry cutter to cut out rounds of the lime cream custard. Place 3 carrot slices on each plate; use a spatula to remove the custard shapes from the dish carefully and place 1 on top of each carrot slice. Place a second carrot slice on top of each piece of lime custard cream. Sprinkle with the vanilla flavoured sauce and decorate with shredded fresh lemon balm leaves.

> Carrots are used in sweet dishes in several parts of the world (in carrot halva in India and in carrot cake in the United States). In this recipe, cooking them in sugar syrup gives them added sweetness. This is quite a complicated dessert and calls for some dexterity but your guests will find it intriguing and delicious.

Frozen chocolate mousse, lemon-flavoured almond brittle, whipped yoghurt

To serve 12

12 tart rings, 6 cm (2½ in) in diameter

For the chocolate mousse

250 ml (9 fl oz) sugar syrup at 30 °C: 300 g (10½ oz) caster sugar and 500 ml (18 fl oz) water

8 egg yolks

250 g (9 oz) couverture chocolate containing at least 64% cocoa solids (see note)

50 ml (2 fl oz) whipping cream, whisked until stiff

For the lemon almond brittle

500 g (17 oz) almond brittle

1 tbsp pure lemon essence

For the tuiles

100 g (3½ oz) butter, softened at room temperature

100 g (3½ oz) caster sugar

100 g (3½ oz) cassonade (raw, unrefined cane sugar)

100 ml (3½ fl oz) orange juice

75 g (2½ oz) plain flour

For the chocolate coating

250 g (9 oz) dark couverture chocolate (see note at end of method)

250 g (9 oz) cocoa butter

Serving and decoration

500 ml (18 fl oz) thick Greek-style yoghurt

full-cream milk

pure cocoa powder

Chocolate mousse

Bring the syrup to the boil over a gentle heat. Use a Kenwood type mixer, with the large bowl in place and fit the whisk attachment. Beat the egg yolks until they are very creamy; keep the whisk attachment rotating at high speed and pour the syrup onto the eggs in a thin, continuous stream. Keep beating until the mixture has cooled completely. While this is in progress, melt the chocolate over hot water or in the microwave oven and stir into the cooled egg and sugar mixture. Fold in 1 tablespoon of the stiffly beaten cream, then fold in the remaining cream.

Lemon almond brittle

Break up the almond brittle or praline into small pieces and add just enough very hot water to melt it, forming a thick sauce. Heat gently in a heavy-bottomed saucepan if necessary. Stir in the lemon essence.

Tuiles

Preheat the oven to 180 °C (gas mark 6). Beat the butter and sugar until pale and creamy; stir in the cassonade sugar, followed by the orange juice. Sift in the flour and fold into the mixture. Have ready a baking sheet covered with silicone baking paper or non-stick greaseproof paper. Spread the mixture out as evenly as possible over the paper and bake in the oven until it is very pale golden brown. Working quickly, while the sheet is still hot, cut it into fairly large triangles and wrap these hot triangles around a rolling pin or similarly shaped utensil. Leave to cool.

Assembling and serving

Place the tart rings on a non-stick baking sheet and fill with the chocolate mixture; freeze until solid. Use a sharp-edged teaspoon to scoop out a small depression in the centre of each and, using a forcing bag and nozzle, fill with some of the lemon almond brittle sauce. Mask this addition with a thin layer of the scooped-out chocolate mixture. Return to. the freezer. Make the chocolate coating: melt the chocolate with the cocoa butter over hot water in a double boiler or in the microwave oven. Take the chocolate mousse rounds out of their moulds and coat with the melted chocolate mixture as evenly as possible. Place in the refrigerator.

Beat the Greek yoghurt with a little milk, until it barely holds its shape. Place a frozen chocolate mousse in the centre of each plate. Put a tuile on top to decorate. Surround with the yoghurt. Sift a little cocoa powder around the edge of the dish.

> If you cannot buy *couverture* chocolate (see note on page 110), buy the best baker's chocolate (*chocolat patissier*) that you can find, with the highest possible cocoa solids content. Menier dark chocolate, preferably unsweetened, is a suitable substitute. You may find coating the chocolate mousse rounds with chocolate difficult; in a professional kitchen, this is done with a special spray-gun utensil. Alternatively, dust the rounds with a little cocoa powder.

White chocolate and coconut ice cream, caramel ice lollies, chocolate sauce

For the coconut dacquoise base

Preheat the oven to 180 °C (gas mark 6). Whisk the egg whites until stiff, add the caster sugar and continue beating until the meringue is very firm. Keep whisking as you add the grated coconut, the icing sugar and, finally, the sifted flour. Spread the meringue mixture out on a sheet of non-stick greaseproof paper on a baking sheet in an even layer approximately 2 cm (¾ in) deep. Smooth the surface with a palette knife and bake in the oven for 15 minutes or until the dacquoise meringue is firm. Transfer to a rack and leave to cool. When cold, use an 8 cm (3–3¼ in) pastry cutter to cut out into discs.

White chocolate and coconut ice

Beat the whipping cream until it stands up in firm peaks. Break the white chocolate up into very small, evenly sized pieces and place in a large mixing bowl. Heat the coconut milk until almost boiling and pour it over the white chocolate; mix well with a spatula until the mixture is very smooth. Stir in the Malibu liqueur and keep stirring continuously as the mixture cools to lukewarm: fold in the whisked cream. Transfer the white chocolate and coconut milk mixture to dome-shaped moulds (*mini-bombes*), preferably flexible; ideally, these should have a diameter of 8 cm (3–3¼ in) so that they will sit neatly on top of the meringue discs. Freeze the white chocolate ice cream 'bombes'. When they have frozen hard, melt the dark chocolate. Turn the white chocolate 'domes' out of their moulds and cover them with the melted chocolate (do this after anchoring them to the meringue bases with a dab of the melted chocolate). Transfer to the refrigerator.

Caramel-coconut ice lollies

Break open the coconut and scrape off the thin brownish inner layer. Cut out the white flesh and grate it finely. Using a small ice-cream scoop, shape 12 small balls of caramel ice cream. Push a lollipop stick securely into each ball and return to the freezer. Take them out of the freezer, check that the sticks are securely frozen in place and roll them in the grated coconut. Return to the freezer again.

Chocolate sauce

Bring the water and sugar to the boil to make a syrup. Stir in the cocoa powder thoroughly; cook for 5 minutes and then stir in the butter. Chill in the refrigerator.

Assembling the dessert

Place a frozen chocolate mousse on its base of meringue in the centre of each plate; add 2 ice lollies and a trickle of the chocolate sauce.

> You will need to work out a timetable when preparing this dessert: the finished ice-cream bombes should not have to wait too long in the refrigerator, but they should not be served deep-frozen, rock-hard. The refrigerator ice box can be used as a halfway house if needed.

For the coconut
dacquoise
450 g (1 lb) egg whites
(approximately 14 medium-sized egg whites)
225 g (½ lb) caster sugar
450 g (1 lb) freshly grated
coconut
225 g (½ lb) icing sugar
75 g (2½ oz) plain flour

For the frozen chocolate
and coconut milk mousses
500 ml (18 fl oz) whipping
cream
300 g (11 oz) white chocolate
100 g (3½ oz) fresh or tinned
coconut milk
100 ml (3½ fl oz) Malibu
liqueur (rum and coconut
milk flavour)
200 g (7 oz) dark, best quality
cooking chocolate

For the coconut-coated
caramel ice-cream lollies
1 coconut
1 litre (1¾ pints) best quality
caramel ice cream
12 lollipop sticks

For the chocolate sauce
250 ml (9 fl oz) water
150 g (5 oz) caster sugar
75 g (2½ oz) pure cocoa
powder
30 g (1 oz) unsalted butter

175

Fritters with sweet pumpkin filling, ice cream, lemon rosemary sauce

To serve 8–10

1 litre (1¾ pints) oil for frying

For the brioche dough
25 g (1 oz) fresh yeast
a little warm milk
500 g (1 lb 2 oz) plain white flour
50 g (2 oz) caster sugar
5 g (scant 1 tsp) salt
5 eggs
250 g (9 oz) butter, at room temperature
1 egg, beaten with 2 tsps cold water, to glaze

For the pumpkin filling
400 g (14 oz) pumpkin flesh
500 ml (18 fl oz) water
100 ml (3½ fl oz) milk
100 g (3½ oz) caster sugar

For the ice cream
1½ litres (2½ pints) full-cream milk
75 g (2½ oz) caster sugar

For the rosemary and lemon sauce
2 lemons
500 ml (18 fl oz) water
300 g (11 oz) caster sugar
1 sprig of fresh rosemary

To assemble and decorate
caster sugar for dusting the fritters
1 dessertspoon of ground cinnamon

Sweet yeast bun dough

Mix the yeast with a little warm milk. Leave to stand for 5 minutes.

Sift the flour with the sugar and salt into a large mixing bowl, forming a mound. Make a well in the centre and into it pour the yeast solution and the eggs. Use your hand to stir andincorporate all the ingedients; knead the dough until it is smooth, elastic and comes away from the sides of the bowl. If you have a large electric mixer with a dough hook you can knead the dough mechanically.

Add the butter, cut into small pieces, and work this into the dough. Leave to 'rest' for about 30 minutes, then knead again (if using a mixer, do this at medium speed). When the dough forms a ball and leaves the sides of the bowl cleanly, place in a large, clean bowl in a warm (not hot) place and leave to rise for 1½ hours.

When the dough has doubled in size, knock it down again. Wrap it in plastic food wrap and chill in the least cold part of the refrigerator.

Sweet pumpkin filling

Cook the pumpkin flesh for approximately 20 minutes in the boiling water, milk and sugar. Drain well and reduce to a thick puree, adding a little of the cooking liquid if it is too thick to process until smooth. Chill in the refrigerator.

Ice cream

Mix the milk and sugar in a saucepan. Heat and simmer until reduced to 500 ml (18 fl oz). Chill overnight, then freeze in an ice-cream maker.

Rosemary and lemon sauce

Peel the lemons with a very sharp serrated knife or patent peeler. Cook the lemons with the sugar and water for 1 hour over a gentle heat. Drain the lemons and process them until smooth in the blender, adding some of the warm syrup to make a pouring sauce. Add the rosemary. Chill in the refrigerator.

Frying the fritters

Take a forcing bag and smooth nozzle and fill two-thirds full with the pumpkin puree. Divide the sweet yeast dough in half. Roll out one half into a sheet approximately 3 mm (⅛ in) thick and brush the entire upper surface with the egg yolk and water mixture. Pipe 'blobs' of puree on the dough sheet. Roll out the remaining dough into a sheet and use it to cover the first sheet. Use a finger to press very lightly around the mounds to make the dough sheets stick together. Using a 5 cm (2 in) diameter plain pastry cutter cut out little 'pies' of dough and filling. Leave to rest for 15 minutes while heating the frying oil to 160 °C. Fry the fritters until they are golden brown.

To serve

Roll the drained fritters in the caster sugar, previously mixed with the ground cinnamon. Serve while hot, accompanied by the ice cream in separate glass dishes and hand the sauce round separately.

> These quantities are large, assuming that you will be making these fritters for a special occasion, such as a child's birthday party. If you are catering for 5–6 people, for a dessert, halve these quantities.

Appendices

List of recipes by chapter

Tastes of the Orient and colours of Asia   p. 119

Index of recipes

Photographic credits

All the photographs in this book were taken by Bernhard Winkelman with the following exceptions:
Olivier Maynard: p. 6, 7, 12, 14 (below right & above left), 16-17, 27, 58-59, 118-119.
Olivier Thieule: Cover image (front flap), p. 11.
Didier Barthélémy: p. 14 (above right).
Marc Walter: p. 44, 47, 91, 161.
Vérascopes Richard-Photothèque Hachette: p. 28, 74, 93, 103, 134, 158.
Agence Top: p. 43 (Jean-Daniel Sudres), 73 (Christine Fleurent).
Agence Rapho: p. 26 (Xavier Desmer), 101 (R. & S. Michaud), 133 (Gérard Sioen),
157 (Mike Yamashita).
Copyright: p. 2-3.

Acknowledgements

Jacques & Laurent Pourcel and Olivier Château would like to thank the following:
Thierry for all the time he spent compiling the recipes.
Valérie and Bernard for their time and their creativity.
Christophe for creating the desserts for their photo call!
Denis, Élie, Ruddy, Nicolas and Nathalie for their indispensable help.
A particular mention for our good friend Philippe Lamboley, for launching the project.
Sophie, Marie-Pierre, Catherine, Brigitte…well done, girls!
Xav and Fred…Keep going…there's still a long way ahead of us!
Our thanks also go to Stephen and to everyone who believes in us!

Valérie Lhomme's is very grateful to the Lluck boutique in Montpellier, AZA (faiences – china and earthenware) and Reine de Saba for all their kind help.

The editor would like to thank Madame Figaro magazine for allowing us to reproduce the photograph on page 85 and also thanks Charlotte Buch-Muller for her invaluable help and her meticulous checking of the text.

Printed in Singapore by Tien Wah Press